Help for Therapists (and their Clients) in dealing with affairs

Based on the results of a survey
of 1,083 people whose spouses had affairs

Peggy Vaughan

Dialog Press
San Diego, CA

ISBN 978-0-936390-20-8

Manufactured in the United States of America

For information about Peggy's work,
visit her website: www.dearpeggy.com

Professional Endorsements

I think this book is nothing short of magnificent. It confirms everything that my patients have taught me over the last 28 years. I think it is a must for those who have experienced an affair, and equally important for those who treat affairs. For therapists, the page on patients' advice to them is worth the price of the book.

Don-David Lusterman, Ph.D.
Author of "Infidelity: A Survival Guide"

You have written a terrific resource for the lay public and therapists alike. What an effective use of quotes. And I value the data about dissatisfaction with therapists; it's such a crap shoot for people seeking help. Your comments about how marital therapists ignore the affair were quite telling. Congratulations on an important public service.

William J. Doherty, Ph.D.
Director of the Marriage and Family Therapy Program
Department of Family Social Science
University of Minnesota

Table of Contents

Overview of Major Points - and Direct Quotes of Responses to question:
"How could therapists be more effective in dealing with affairs?"
> Deal directly with the affair, not just ordinary marriage counseling
> Deal with the emotional impact of the affair.
> Don't "blame" the affair on the hurt spouse.
> Be supportive of those couples who want to try to save the marriage.
> Don't keep secrets or too quickly believe lies of the one who had an affair.
> See both parties together.
> Be aware of the impact of your gender/beliefs/experience on therapy.
> Don't expect the hurt party to forget the affair or "set it aside and go on."
> Help clients connect with others who have "been there."
> Be well-informed about affairs and provide good information.
> Encourage honest communication and answering all questions.
> Miscellaneous Comments about Therapists

Acknowledgments

First, I want to thank the 1,083 men and women who participated in this research. My gratitude goes to each of them for honestly sharing their personal experiences with this issue. I have a great deal of admiration and respect for their willingness to help others learn more about dealing with a spouse's affair.

I also want to express my appreciation to John Gottman for initially suggesting that I undertake this study and for supporting my effort by discussing the goals for the survey as well as providing the appropriate form for collecting the demographic information.

Finally, I want to thank all the people who have shared their lives with me since 1980 when I first began trying to provide more information, understanding and perspective about the issue of affairs.

I hope the information gained from the responses to this survey will be useful both to those who are currently struggling to recover from a spouse's affair as well as those who may face this crisis in the future. And I hope the "Advice" from the respondents will enable therapists to be more effective in their work with clients who are struggling with this devastating experience.

Introduction

While Therapists and their Clients are the "target audience" for this book, I hope it will be widely read by those whose lives have not yet been touched by affairs.

Here is an excerpt from my book *The Monogamy Myth* explaining "Why it's Everybody's Business."

"The most immediate reason we need to be informed about affairs is because no one is immune from having affairs disrupt their lives or the lives of those they care about; they happen to all kinds of people, in all walks of life. Traditionally our attitude has been that unless it touches us personally, we deal with it by ignoring it, denying it, or condemning it. Unfortunately, this does nothing either to help deter affairs or to deal with their consequences. If we're to be the kind of caring, compassionate society we aspire to be, we can't turn our backs on the countless people who are suffering alone."

The isolation with which so many people struggle with this issue allows them to feel that it's *only* "personal." I'm convinced that this is much more than just a personal issue; it touches the lives of almost everyone in some way—so it needs and deserves more responsible attention within society as a whole.

Here is a quote from one of the many messages I have received through the years that makes a plea for more widespread attention to dealing with this painful issue.

"Before I joined BAN I thought that all the problems we faced were personal to us and solely a product of our relationship. I now see that so many of our behaviors and feelings are common to other marriages where affairs have come in to create havoc (from the pain of the one whose partner has affairs to the tendency to rationalize on the part of the spouse). If it is the case that this situation is commonplace, how come everyone isn't talking about it? How come we aren't taught about it in sex education classes, in Sunday school, on the lap of our grandmother...? Why aren't the sociologists and psychologists researching it more - God knows they research every other facet of human behavior! Open any glossy magazine and you will find numerous articles about keeping your sex life vibrant, communication, etc., etc., but nothing about what really happens in affairs."

Note: BAN (referenced in the above quote) refers to "Beyond Affairs Network," a Support Group I founded many years ago.

I hope this study will help bring more attention to this issue and more understanding of its impact on those who face this devastating experience. I also hope it will contribute toward Breaking the Code of Secrecy about affairs. Please read the article titled *Breaking the Code of Secrecy* that is posted on my Website: www.dearpeggy.com

Basic Information about the Survey

(Including Notes about the Sample and the Collection Process)

This is a report on the results of a Survey on Extramarital Affairs that I conducted through my Website (www.dearpeggy.com) in which I sought information from those whose spouses had had affairs.

Here's the offer I extended when I posted the Questionnaire on the Website:

If you have ever had a spouse who had an extramarital affair…
We invite you to participate (anonymously) in this study.

Of those who responded to the survey, 75% were women and 25% were men, all of whose spouses had had an extramarital affair. For a breakdown of the responses by gender, refer to Appendix III.

In addition to gathering demographic information and establishing the current status of their marriage and whether they had children, each participant answered 35 multiple-choice questions about various aspects of their experience.

The size of the sample was 1,083. The number in the sample was reduced from the 1,189 responses submitted, using the following process:

—We first checked ISP (Internet Service Provider) addresses to remove duplicates, avoiding more than one submission by an individual. (Based on checking age, gender, etc., we did not remove submissions that were clearly from a different person simply using the same computer.)

—We then removed those who answered questions both about "staying married" and about "getting divorced"—as well as those who answered neither of these sets of questions. (These may have been submitted by people in committed relationships who were not married—but this study was limited only to married men and women whose spouse had an affair.)

Since the usefulness of the data depends on having complete responses to all the questions, only those questionnaires filled out in full are included in these results.

Upon submission of the completed questionnaire, each participant was invited to add their Comments. The specific question they were asked to address was:

"How could therapists be more effective in dealing with affairs?"

The responses to this question have been organized into 12 major categories and are included later in this report as "Advice from Respondents to Therapists."

Help for Therapists

Note: Following the section containing "Advice for Therapists" is a collection of additional comments that were submitted on Other Topics. These also provide invaluable insights into effectively dealing with the issue of affairs.

(NOTE: The entire Questionnaire is included in Appendix I.)

Overview of the Demograhic Information

Age: 76% of the sample are between ages 30 and 50.

Gender: 25% of the sample are men; 75% are women.

Country of Residence: 90% are from the USA.

Ethnic or Racial Group Membership: 91% are of White, non-Hispanic Origin

Religious Affiliation: 73% are Christian (30% Catholicism, 43% Protestantism)

Education: 60% have up to 4 years college, 26% have graduate education/degrees

Income: 54% earn between $20,000 and $60,000

Occupation: 33% professional, 28% clerical or managerial, 12% full-time homemaker

(NOTE: The complete Demographic Information is included in Appendix II.)

Other Information about the Respondents

Current status of marriage to spouse who had affair(s)

76% - married and living together

9% - married but not living together

2% - legally separated

13% - divorced

There's a popular assumption that affairs usually lead to divorce. This may be because there's less likelihood of openly discussing this experience when couples stay married as compared to when they divorce. However, this result is consistent with the information I have received from people during the past 30 years.

Child (or children) with spouse who had affair(s)

77% - Yes

23% - No

The presence of children in a marriage (being a parent) does not appear to represent a deterrent to the incidence of affairs. It may, however, be a factor in the report by 76% of the respondents that they are still married.

Similarities of responses by men and women

Note the identical responses to the question about the current status of marriage to spouse who had affair(s).

Men – 76% still married and living together

Women – 76% still married and living together

Many people assume that there are significant differences in the reactions of men and women to a spouse's affair—but their reactions are far more similar than generally recognized. One of the most common misconceptions is that men are much more likely to get a divorce when their wife has an affair. But, as indicated above, the same percentage of men and women reported they are still married and living with the spouse who had affair(s).

I anticipated this similarity based on the information I have received through the years. (During the past decade, about 40% of the people I've heard from have been men whose wives had affairs.) Since men may be less likely to acknowledge that they have faced this situation, people are more likely to hear about those who do get a divorce—and falsely assume that they are representative of the way *most* men react.

(NOTE: All Responses Broken Down by Gender are included in Appendix III.)

Methods of Analysis

Statistical Analyses

Statistical analyses (with Chi-square statistics) were used to test 8 specific hypotheses regarding the association between honest communication and recovery/rebuilding trust—using questions about recovery as dependent variables and questions about honest communication as independent variables.

(These statistical analyses are reported in the following section.)

Simple Percentages

All of the responses were also calculated using simple percentages.

(The responses to all 35 of the multiple-choice questions are provided following the report of the statistical analyses.)

Statistical Analyses

(Focusing on the Significance of Talking)

The following Statistical Analyses represent the most significant results of this survey. In fact, the primary purpose in conducting the survey was to investigate the reliability of the information I have consistently received through the years: *that honest communication is key to personally recovering and to maintaining and rebuilding the marriage*. It is satisfying to see that these results indicate a strong association between honest communication and whether marriages survive and individuals recover.

Goals of the Survey

- To discover the factors involved in whether or not marriages are likely to survive.

- To determine the factors involved in whether or not people are likely to personally recover from this experience.

General Hypotheses

- Higher levels of honest communication increase the likelihood of maintaining and rebuilding the marriage.

- Higher levels of honest communication increase the likelihood of recovering from a spouse's affair(s).

Statistical Results of 8 Hypotheses

The analyses of the results indicate:

- The amount the affair was discussed with the spouse and the extent to which the spouse answered questions were significantly associated with the current marital status and quality of the marriage.

- The amount the affair was discussed with the spouse and the extent to which the spouse answered questions were significantly associated with recovery.

Below are the Results of 8 hypotheses shown to be "statistically significant" with a p value of $<.001$ (statistical significance being defined by p values less than .05).

1. Hypothesis: A couple is more likely to stay married when they thoroughly discuss the whole situation.

x^2 *(2, N = 1083) = 78.30,* p *<.001*

55% of those who discussed the situation very little were still married (and living together)

78% of those who discussed the situation a good bit were still married (and living together)

86% of those who discussed the situation a lot were still married (and living together)

The amount that the affair was discussed with the partner was significantly associated with present marital status.

2. Hypothesis: A couple is more likely to stay married when the spouse answers their questions.

x^2 *(2, N = 1083) = 66.58,* p *<.001*

59% of those who refused to answer questions were still married (and living together)

81% of those whose partner answered some of their questions were still married (and living together)

86% of those whose partner answered all their questions were still married (and living together)

The extent to which the partner answered questions was significantly associated with present marital status.

3. Hypothesis: They are more likely to have healed when they thoroughly discuss the whole situation.

x^2 *(4, N = 1083) = 33.27, p <.001*

35% of those who discussed the situation very little felt somewhat or mostly healed

51% of those who discussed the situation a good bit felt somewhat or mostly healed

54% of those who discussed the situation a lot felt somewhat or mostly healed

The amount that the affair was discussed with the partner was significantly associated with the degree to which they had healed.

4. Hypothesis: They are more likely to have healed when their spouse answers their questions.

x^2 *(4, N = 1083) = 37.99,* p *<.001*

41% of those whose partner refused to answer questions felt somewhat or mostly healed

51% of those whose partner answered some their questions felt somewhat or mostly healed

55% of those whose partner answered all their questions felt somewhat or mostly healed

The extent to which the partner answered questions was significantly associated with the degree to which they had healed.

5. Hypothesis: Trust is more likely to be rebuilt when they thoroughly discuss the whole situation.

x^2 (4, N = 825) = 34.13, *p* <.001

32% of those who discussed the situation very little rebuilt some trust

42% of those who discussed the situation a good bit rebuilt some trust

58% of those who discussed the situation a lot rebuilt some trust

The amount that the affair was discussed with the partner was significantly associated with rebuilding trust (among those who are still married).

6. Hypothesis: Trust is more likely to be rebuilt when the spouse answers their questions.

x^2 *(4, N = 825) = 79.54,* p *<.001*

31% of those whose partner refused to answer questions rebuilt some trust

43% of those who discussed the situation a good bit rebuilt some trust

72% of those whose partner answered all their questions rebuilt some trust

The extent to which the partner answered questions was significantly associated with rebuilding trust (among those who are still married).

7. Hypothesis: The relationship is more likely to be "improved" compared to pre-affair days when they thoroughly discuss the whole situation.

x^2 *(4, N = 825) = 56.39*, p *<.001*

21% of relationships where they discussed the situation very little were better than before the affair(s)

43% of relationships where they discussed the situation a good bit were better than before the affair(s)

59% of relationships where they discussed the situation a lot were better than before the affair(s)

The extent to which they discussed the situation was significantly associated with the degree to which the relationship "improved" compared to pre-affair days (among those who are still married).

8. Hypothesis: The relationship is more likely to be "improved" compared to pre-affair days when the spouse answers their questions.

x^2 *(4, N = 825) = 59.99*, p *<.001*

30% of relationships where partner refused to answer questions were better than before the affair(s)

45% of relationships where partner answered some questions were better than before the affair(s)

65% of relationships where partner answered all questions were better than before the affair(s)

The extent to which the partner answered questions was significantly associated with the degree to which the relationship "improved" compared to pre-affair days (among those who are still married).

Significance of the Results of the Statistical Analyses

In the past, there has been a general assumption that it's not helpful to "tell" much about the affair or to talk much about what happened. So there's still a great reluctance on the part of those who have had affairs to answer questions and to continue talking about the whole situation.

Unfortunately, a large segment of the therapeutic community has reinforced the idea that it's not wise to ask too many questions or do too much talking about the affair. The rationale is that the more a spouse knows, the greater the pain. However, this thinking is contradicted by the results of this Survey.

The findings clearly show the importance of "telling." Getting answers to questions and thoroughly discussing the details of the affair *increase* the likelihood of maintaining and rebuilding the marriage and *increase* the likelihood of recovering from a spouse's affair.

These survey results are consistent with what I have been told repeatedly through the years: "nothing is worse than not knowing." For a more thorough discussion of this "Need to Know," see the article by this title on my Website listed under "Articles about Affairs."

I hope the statistical data reported above—demonstrating the connection between honest communication and both staying married and recovering—will help the professional community (and all those struggling to deal with this issue) better understand the importance of answering questions and thoroughly discussing the entire situation.

Responses to the 35 Multiple-Choice Questions

(Including my Commentary about the Responses)

All questions with an * were required to be answered in order to be included in the survey. (Therefore, all questions followed by an * had 1,083 Responses. Others are as noted.)

All responses were based on the first marriage in which a spouse had an affair.

All responses were based on the first time they learned that an affair(s) took place.

The Period During Courtship and Early Years of Marriage:

How long did you date your spouse prior to marriage? *

24% - Less than a year

65% - One to 5 years

11% - More than 5 years

Results: Time spent dating does not determine whether there will be an affair.

The above responses can be misleading if they are taken to mean that a marriage based on a courtship of "one to 5 years" (65%) is more susceptible to affairs than one of "less than a year" (24%). This is more likely a reflection of the fact that more people date "one to 5 years" before marrying than those who date "less than a year" before marrying. The same factor is probably at work regarding the report of 11% dating "more than 5 years" in that fewer people may date that long prior to marriage.

Although the responses may simply reflect the percentages who date various periods prior to marriage, there is nevertheless a significant underlying message: that all marriages are vulnerable to affairs—regardless of the length of the courtship period or the degree to which they "got to know each other" prior to marriage.

That's because it's unreasonable to assume that the beliefs, values and intentions of the individuals at the time of marriage will be maintained throughout the rest of the marriage. People often change their attitudes about various issues as they proceed through life, sometimes in ways that are positive and sometimes in ways that are negative.

Obviously, any change that leads to having an affair is negative. However, it's not that changes in values or attitudes inevitably lead to this kind of behavior. It's just that any such changes a person *fails to share* with their partner leaves them vulnerable to getting "carried away" with the fantasy/fun/excitement of an affair in a way that would be unlikely if they maintained open communication.

In the final analysis, it's the dishonesty and deception that is most instrumental in people pursuing their fantasies rather than the attraction or temptation per se. So it points to the importance of keeping open the lines of communication about *all* significant issues, including monogamy and how to deal with attractions to others.

How did you (as a couple) deal with attractions to others? *

　15% - Were not attracted to others

　65% - Didn't discuss attractions

　20% - Talked openly about attractions

Results: Attractions are normal – so it's important to talk about how to deal with them.

It's normal to feel attractions to other people—no matter how much you love your spouse or how much your spouse loves you. While it's probably something you don't want to think about, understanding that attractions to others are normal can be the first step toward being able to keep them in perspective. If you see attractions as a direct threat to your love (thinking that if you and your partner love each other, you will never be attracted to anyone else), you're granting power to attractions that they would not otherwise possess.

The 15% indicating they "were not attracted to others" is reflective of the tendency to deny the reality of attractions—and the failure to recognize that attractions are not, in and of themselves, the problem. The problem comes when they are acted on. And the best way to decrease the likelihood of that happening is to honestly discuss this issue and your feelings about it on an ongoing basis.

If you try to deny the possibility of attractions, you send a subtle (or not so subtle) signal that you don't want to know about any feelings of attraction your spouse might have toward others. You're in essence sending a message that says, "Lie to me; pretend you're never attracted to anyone else." This, of course, causes other problems related to honesty that can have serious consequences for your relationship.

Attractions become a much greater threat to the relationship whenever acknowledging them is taboo. (Note the 65% who said they "didn't discuss attractions.") If you can't talk about these feelings, they become your own private secret and are likely to grow in intensity and desire. But openly discussing your feelings brings a degree of reality to the issue that leads to a more sensible and responsible way of thinking, which in turn reduces the desire to act on the attractions. While it seems scary at first, talking honestly about your attractions and how to deal with them actually reduces their power. Talking also reduces the danger of *acting* on the attractions. (Note that only 20% of the respondents said they "talked openly about attractions.")

How did you as a couple deal with the issue of monogamy? *

    50% - Assumed monogamy without discussing it

    31% - Talked about it early in relationship, but did not continue to discuss it

    19% - Had ongoing discussions about our commitment to monogamy

Results: Monogamy cannot be assumed; it requires ongoing honesty discussion.

People tend to think that the marriage vows offer some kind of "guarantee" of monogamy—that they can simply "assume" monogamy without discussing it. (This was the case with 50% of those who responded.) However, even if a person *intends* to be monogamous when they get married, it doesn't mean they won't change their thinking at some future time. So monogamy doesn't depend on a one-time decision (or one-time discussion as indicated by the 31% who "talked about it early in relationship but did not continue to discuss it"). When there's only a promise of monogamy, there's no way to determine when a person's thinking is changing and they are moving toward the possibility of an affair. (Only 19% of the respondents "had ongoing discussions about our commitment to monogamy.") This result (that people tend to believe the "myth" that you can *assume* monogamy without discussing it) reflects one of the main points I have made for the past twenty years, as reflected in the title of my book *The Monogamy Myth*.

The Period When the Affair(s) was Taking Place:

Did you suspect an affair? *

    33% - Had no suspicions

    42% - Had slight suspicion, but didn't focus on it

    25% - Intensely suspicious

Results: It's common to ignore or deny fears/suspicions—because we don't want it to be true.

The largest group of respondents (42%) report having "slight suspicion, but didn't focus on it." People tend to rationalize their early suspicions of an affair because they don't *want* to believe it's true. The sense of personal shame and embarrassment that comes with entertaining the possibility that this could happen causes them to ignore or deny their suspicions. In fact, denying their suspicions (even to themselves) may be reflected in the 33% who said they "had no suspicions." On the other hand, when they're open to picking up the cues of an affair, they're likely to be "intensely suspicious," as reported by 25% of the respondents.

What was the primary factor that might have warranted suspicion? *

    33% - Gut feeling/intuition that something was wrong

    44% - Changes in spouse's attitudes and/or behavior

    23% - Information I discovered or others told me

Results: Suspicions that arise in various ways can be equally valid.

The first level of suspicion is that "gut feeling" that something is wrong. (33% of the respondents indicated this sensing.) But many people, after discovering an affair, can look back and recognize that they had this kind of feeling. For instance, the 44% whose suspicion was based on "changes in spouse's attitudes and/or behavior" may have also had the gut feeling about the meaning of the behavior. However, many people feel a need for "information" to verify their suspicions (as was the case with 23% of the respondents).

Did you confront your spouse about your suspicion? *

    24% - No

    35% - Yes, but in a somewhat tentative or casual way

    41% - Yes, very strongly and/or persistently

Results: Whether and how to confront usually depends on the strength of the desire to know.

Often, even when there are strong suspicions, there's a hesitancy to confront the spouse in a timely and effective way—because there's such a strong hope that the suspicions are not true. And many attempts at confrontation are really thinly-disguised pleas for *reassurance* instead of a genuine desire to know the truth, regardless of what it may be. So a person needs to be sure they really want the truth before confronting their partner. The 24% who answered "No" regarding confronting their spouse may be among those who didn't *really* want to know. This ambivalence about "wanting to know" is further reflected by the 35% who confronted in a "somewhat tentative or casual way." This may also be tied to the lack of "proof" and a reluctance to trust their gut instincts as to what is happening. The 41% who "strongly and/or persistently" confronted may have been clearer about *wanting* the truth and felt more prepared to *face* the truth. However, no matter when, why, or how a confrontation takes place, the most common response by the spouse who is confronted is *denial*—which, of course, can be extremely frustrating and confusing.

The Discovery of the Affair(s):

How did you find out about the affair(s)? *

33% - Spouse voluntarily told me

14% - Someone else told me

53% - I "found out" on my own

Results: "Never Tell" is the motto of most people having affairs.

Most people having affairs go to great lengths to prevent their spouses from every finding out. So the responses by the 33% who said their "spouse voluntarily told me" may be misleading in that there was no category for "Spouse finally told me after repeated questioning and intense pressure." Actually, this 33% is made up of all those who were NOT told by someone else and who did NOT find out of their own; so it includes both those who "voluntarily" *offered* the information as well as those who provided the information under pressure and questioning. The 53% who found out on their own reflects the enormous "need to know" that motivates people to do everything possible to discover the truth when it is not acknowledged upon confrontation. And for some people this prior independent verification of their suspicions is an essential prerequisite to preparing for a confrontation.

How long ago did you find out? *

47% - Less than 1 year ago

38% - One to 5 years ago

15% - More than 5 years ago

Results: It takes a long time to come to grips with the reality of a spouse's affair.

It's understandable that so many of the respondents (47%) were people who found out less than a year ago—since the immediate need for help/insight/understanding is usually strongest in the beginning. However, it's significant that all other respondents found out about the affair more than a year prior to responding to this survey. The fact that they were visiting my website after this much time had passed illustrates how this experience continues to be a problem for a long time. (As I will discuss later, I've never seen anyone completely recover from the emotional impact of a spouse's affair in less than two years.)

*How long had you been married when you found out? *

23% - Less than 5 years

39% - Five to 15 years

38% - More than 15 years

Results: Affairs can happen at any point in the marriage.

There's a tendency to believe that there's a special point in a marriage when affairs are more likely—like the "7-year itch" or the more recent focus on a "4-year itch." However, through the years I have gathered other data on the length of the marriage at the time an affair was discovered, and found that affairs happen in marriages of *any* length—from 2 years to 39 years (and even occasionally from the very beginning of the marriage or after 40 or more years). There's never a point at which it's reasonable to assume this "can't happen."

*How long had the affair(s) been taking place when you found out? *

69% - Less than a year

23% - One to 5 years

8% - More than 5 years

Results: Most affairs last less than 2 years and most are discovered while still in progress.

The early stages of an affair are the time of greatest intensity (and whatever changes take place in the spouse's attitude or behavior are more obvious at that time), so it's understandable that most affairs are discovered during this initial phase. (60% of the respondents said the affair had been taking place less than a year.) Most affairs don't last beyond two years, mainly because that's how long it takes for the initial euphoria/infatuation to cool down to where it loses some of its fantasy status. Once an affair has ended, it's less likely to be discovered. Of course, a person who feels they have "successfully" had an affair (meaning they did it "without getting caught") is more likely to engage in future affairs. And the false sense of security they feel the next time around may lead them to take more risks, eventually causing them to get caught.

How many affairs did you find out about? *

   69% - One

   25% - Two to 5

   6% - More than 5

Results: The first affair that is discovered is not necessarily the first affair that has happened.

At first glance, it might seem reassuring that 69% of the respondents said there was only one affair. However, the question was carefully worded to reflect how many affairs they "found out about"—not necessarily how many affairs had actually taken place. (A spouse responding to this survey has no way of being absolutely sure how many affairs took place.)

Most people don't get caught in their very first affair—any more than people get a speeding ticket the very first time they speed. Earlier I mentioned that a motto among people having affairs is: *"Never Tell."* Well, the rest of that motto is: *"If questioned, deny it. If caught, say as little as possible."* So most people only tell whatever they feel they *have* to tell, meaning whatever has already been exposed or whatever they think will eventually get exposed or can't be avoided. Getting the "whole truth" is like peeling an onion, with each layer coming off very slowly. And, of course, sometimes the "whole truth" is never revealed.

Talking about the Affairs(s) with Spouse:

How MUCH did you and your spouse discuss the whole situation? *

   20% - Very little

   40% - A good bit, but not as much as I wanted

   40% - A lot

Results: A lot of discussion is wanted/needed by the spouse trying to deal with an affair.

Many people who have had an affair genuinely believe that it's best not to talk too much about the situation. However, almost universally, the spouse wants/needs a LOT of communication.

Here's an excerpt from my book, *The Monogamy Myth*, that describes the "thousands of hours" we spent talking through this whole situation.

> *"I remember how tough it was on my husband when I continually asked more and more questions. Intellectually, I wanted to move on and get over it, but emotionally I needed the ongoing support and understanding he gave me. It was extremely important that he never said, 'enough is enough, let's get on with our lives.' Of course, nobody would choose to go through the thousands of hours of talking about this if there were some other way. In my own case, I think it was an essential part of overcoming my feelings and finding peace of mind."*

How LONG did the talking continue? *

55% - Less than 6 months

34% - Six months to 2 years

11% - More than 2 years

Results: The goal is not to stop talking—but to be able to talk without the painful emotions.

Most people think there should be some kind of time-frame for talking—and that once that time has passed there should be no more talking about this experience. As the above responses reflect, more than half the respondents talked for less than 6 months, with a steady decline after that time. (As mentioned earlier, no one fully recovers in less than 2 years, so this means they're left to deal with this *alone*, making recovery even more difficult.)

Of course, there's nothing *magic* about the 2 years; it's not as if that's the end of the issue. In fact, it's very difficult to integrate any such life-altering experience into the reality of our lives, but that difficulty becomes even greater if the issue is buried rather than dealt with. It's literally "buried alive" and comes back to haunt the individual and the relationship for the rest of their lives.

Was the talking helpful? *

32% - No, we just went over and over the same things

45% - Yes, but didn't resolve as much as I would like

23% - Yes, it was essential to my getting beyond this

Responses to the 35 Multiple-Choice Questions

Results: The quality of the talking is equally as important as the quantity.

Talking just for the sake of talking is not useful. In order for talking to be helpful, it needs to "move the process along," meaning it adds to the overall understanding of the situation. As long as the talking is primarily emotion-driven, there can be little rational thinking or problem-solving. So it's necessary to make a commitment to learning (and using) more effective way of talking.

There are a number of factors that can make a big difference in the effectiveness of the talking, including:
- motive: being motivated by a desire to improve the relationship
- timing: considering the best time to have a conversation
- location: choosing surroundings that support communication
- attitude: having an attitude conducive to a productive discussion
- responsiveness: listening in such a way as to encourage honesty
- expectations: openness to whatever results from this effort

   (Each of these factors is expanded in *The Monogamy Myth*.)

Did you want to know details about the affair(s)? ＊

   7% - No, I didn't want to know details

   31% - Yes, but I wanted only general information (who, when, why)

   62% - Yes, I wanted to know everything, including details

Results: Most people want to know details.

In this survey, 93% of the respondents wanted information, with two-thirds of those wanting to know "everything." Although many people find these Results to be surprising—they were NOT surprising to me because I have consistently heard this same desire from thousands of people during the past 30 years.

Most people having affairs are reluctant to disclose information; in fact, (as mentioned earlier), the common attitude regarding disclosing details is: "if caught say as little as possible." But the above responses (showing the strong desire for knowing details) helps to understand the results showing the positive association between honest communication and recovery/sustaining marriage that were reported in the Statistical Analyses section.

Unfortunately, there has not been a lot of support for sharing details and talking through all the issues surrounding affairs. There has been a false focus on the details themselves, failing to recognize the importance of the *willingness* to be honest. This willingness has a positive impact on recovery and sustaining the marriage because it provides hope for more honesty in the future. (One of the messages I've heard repeatedly through the years is that people recover from the *facts* about the sexual relationship before they recover from the fact that they were *deceived*—so hope for a future without this kind of deception becomes critical.)

One of the reasons for such strong results is the powerful "Need to Know" on the part of the spouse who learns of their partner's affair. When learning of a partner's affair, most people feel an intense need to know—asking questions to try to make some kind of sense out of what has happened. However, there's still a great reluctance on the part of those who have had affairs to answer questions and to continue talking through the entire situation.

While it's important to get answers to your questions IF you ask questions, this does NOT mean you "should" ask questions unless/until you really want to know. It's just that it's essential to get answers if you DO ask. While for most people, "getting answers to your questions" is a key ingredient in rebuilding trust and building a strong marriage, no one should be forced to hear things they don't want to hear. But if they DO want to hear details, they deserve to have their questions answered. As discussed above, it's the willingness of the partner to answer questions that is so critical, not whether or not you *ask* for the answers.

So each person needs to decide for themselves the timing of when/what/how much they want to know. (It's important to determine that you really want the truth, and are not just hoping for some kind of reassurance or disclaimers.) For most people, "not knowing" is worst of all—because their imagination fills in the blanks and the wondering never ceases.

Did your spouse answer your questions? *

    28% - No, refused to talk beyond basics

    49% - Yes, but only told some of the information after much pressure

    23% - Yes, told me everything I wanted to know

Results: Getting answers to questions is one of the most critical factors in recovery/rebuilding.

There's a natural reluctance/resistance on the part of the person who had an affair to answer questions about their experience. This is reflected in the responses showing that only 23% "told me everything I wanted to know." And almost half "only told some of the information after much pressure." However, getting answers to whatever questions they want to ask is a key factor in recovering from this experience and rebuilding the marriage.

Here's an excerpt from *The Monogamy Myth* about why we need answers to our questions:

> *"When a person discovers their mate is having an affair, their world suddenly turns upside down. In order to recover any sense of balance, they need to get more information and understanding of the situation. Without answers to their questions, they convince themselves that the answers must all be bad; otherwise why wouldn't they be told what they want to know. They feel they're being treated like a child, and they resent it.*
>
> *"If the information didn't exist, it wouldn't be so frustrating and demeaning. But they know their partner has it, and simply refuses to give it to them. This makes a balance of power in the relationship impossible... It's doubtful if trust can ever be restored in a relationship where this persists."*

Talking about the Affair(s) with Others:

Who did you talk to? *

14% - No one

41% - Friends/family/others

45% - Professional (counselor/therapist/clergy, etc.)

Results: Most people talk to SOMEONE because the pain is so hard to bear alone.

While the 14% of respondents who spoke to "no one" was a relatively small number, it's still a significant reflection of the secrecy that pervades the issue of affairs. As reflected above, about an even number chose to talk to friends/family and to professionals. It's been my experience that *who* someone talks to is less critical than the fact that they *do* talk to someone instead of trying to deal with this situation in isolation. When something feels "too awful to talk about," it's likely to feel "too awful to get over," so it's important to be able to reach out and talk to someone.

How MUCH did you talk to friends/family/others (NOT including professionals)? *

22% - Not at all

47% - Very limited

31% - A LOT

Results: Simply breaking the silence and secrecy is more important than how much you talk.

As reflected by the fact that most people talked to friends/family in a *very limited* way, the significance of reaching out is based far more on the need to avoid being alone with this knowledge than it is with any specific amount of talking or help that might result. Also, one of the reasons that talking with friends/family may be limited is due to the way some people react. Since friends may feel uneasy about focusing on this issue at all (because they don't want to think it could happen to them—or to anyone they know), they may not be able to be responsive and supportive. And relatives may have trouble dealing with their own personal reactions to the fact that a family member had an affair, leading them to have difficulty in responding to the need to talk through these feelings. The responses to the following question (showing that 50% of friends/family "helped some, but were not as helpful as I'd like") may be a reflection of the factors just described.

Was it helpful to talk to friends/family/others? *

  12% - Didn't talk or not useful

  50% - Helped some, but not as much as I'd like

  38% - Extremely helpful

Results: The most important benefit of talking to friends/family is the process, not the content.

Since 50% found talking to friends/family somewhat helpful and 38% found it extremely helpful, most people (88%) overall found it helpful. This is a dramatic example of the power of *not* being alone. In most instances, the helpfulness does not relate to any *specific* help in terms of "advice." (In fact, too much advice-giving can be a drawback.) The main helpfulness is in being able to open up to someone rather than keeping it all inside. One of the biggest benefits of talking is not in anything related to the other person's *response*; it's simply helpful to try to articulate the feelings enough for someone else to understand. In other words, the process of trying to share the thoughts/feelings in a way that someone else can understand them serves to bring more clarity. When dealing with this alone, the thoughts/ideas tend to slip around inside the head. But organizing your thoughts enough to verbally express them leads to more insight, perspective, and ultimately better decision-making.

Deciding Whether to Stay Married or Get a Divorce:

How long after discovery was there a decision as to whether to stay married or get a divorce? *

56% - Less than 3 months

30% - Three months to a year

14% - More than a year

Results: The decision needs to be based on thoughtful assessment rather than emotional reaction.

The fact that most respondents (56%) made a decision about the fate of the marriage in less than 3 months after discovery reflects the tendency to feel pressure to quickly decide what to do. However, most people are so overcome with emotion during the first few months that any decision reached during that time is unlikely to be based on clear, rational thinking. If at all possible, it's better to remain open to *either* possibility (rebuilding the marriage or divorcing) until after spending time and effort getting more clarity about the prospects for the future of the relationship.

The bottom line is that the decision is best made based on the prospects for the future rather than being based on what happened in the past. Any life crisis (and an affair certainly qualifies as a crisis) "changes the world as we've known it." And it takes time to envision the world based on the new reality—and even more time to reach some understanding of what has happened and what to do about it.

Even if there is a decision to get a divorce at some future time (after investing a lot of effort in determining whether the marriage can be rebuilt), this does not mean that a decision to divorce should have been made earlier. That's because it's not just *what* decision is made—but how well you can *live* with the decision. Those who divorce only after investing lots of time and energy into determining the possibilities for rebuilding the marriage are likely to be able to live with their decision, knowing they did all they could. But those who decide to get out too quickly tend to second-guess themselves and wonder "what if…" or "should I have…"—so they have more difficulty *living* with their decision. Even if the final decision is the same, the process used to reach the decision makes a significant difference.

What was the decision? *

54% - To stay married

19% - To get a divorce

27% - Still undecided

Results: Most people DO stay married.

In the earlier section reporting basic "Information about the respondents," it was noted that 76% reported they are still married and living together. This would indicate that almost all of the 27% who were "still undecided" eventually joined the 54% who made an initial decision to stay married.

There has long been an assumption that most marriages end when an affair is discovered. That assumption is related to the fact that the secrecy surrounding this issue leads us to only hear about affairs in those marriages that end. When couples stay together, they may never share the information about the affair, leaving the general public to falsely assume that most marriages end when there is an affair.

This assumption is further strengthened by the fact that most people will *say*, "if my spouse ever had an affair, I'd get out." But any such comment is meaningless, since nobody knows what they would do unless/until it actually happens to them. At that point, there are many factors, both emotional and practical, that come into consideration.

Your Current Condition
(Regardless of Whether Still Married or Divorced):

Do you still dwell on the affair(s)? *

    55% - Yes, it's still a pain I carry every day

    32% - While I still think about it from time to time, it's not a constant focus

    13% - No, I've pretty much put it in perspective in my life and moved on

Results: It takes time (at least two years) to get beyond the pain of a spouse's affair.

The fact that 55% report that it's "still a pain I carry every day" is predictable in view of the fact that (in a response to an earlier question) 47% found out about the affair "less than 1 year ago" and 38% found out "one to 5 years ago." Since it takes most people at least two years to recover from the emotional impact of their spouse's affair (even when there's a conscientious effort toward recovering), it's almost inevitable that many will "still think about it from time to time." In fact, there's some hopefulness in the fact that 32% report that "it's not a constant focus."

Responses to the 35 Multiple-Choice Questions

Do you feel a sense of forgiveness/resolution? *

34% - No, I still have lots of anger and resentment toward my spouse (or ex-spouse)

56% - I think I've "forgiven," but I don't feel it will ever be completely resolved

10% - Yes, my spouse's behavior since ending the affair has allowed me to let it go

Results: This life-altering experience may never be completely resolved.

Since a partner's affair is a *life-altering event*, it's not surprising that 56% "don't feel it will ever be completely resolved." It's significant that even though most don't feel it's "resolved," they nevertheless think they have "forgiven." And referring again to the earlier responses indicating that it had been "less than a year" for most people, it's interesting that most have already "forgiven." (Of course, reports of forgiveness are usually more a reflection of an *intention* to forgive or a decision to *try* to forgive; true forgiveness is the result of a process that takes much more time.)

Have you healed? *

33% - No, I'm still in great pain

49% - I've healed somewhat but feel I will always carry a scar

18% - I've mostly healed and actually grown in many ways

Results: Healing is more difficult because it's about more than just the affair.

One of the many factors involved in healing (that may be related to the wide range of responses to this question) is whether or not someone believes it's *possible* to heal. (A failure to believe it's possible can become a "self-fulfilling prophesy"—in that failing to believe it's possible to rebuild the marriage can lead to failing to take the steps that might lead to healing).

While it's encouraging to see that a total of 67% report being "somewhat healed" (49%) or "mostly healed" (18%), the fact that almost half feel they will "always carry a scar" is another indication of the lasting impact of this experience. Much of the feeling of "always carrying a scar" may be based on the fact that there's now a totally new reality to their lives that doesn't fit with their previous sense of reality. It's much more than *just* dealing with the affair itself (as if that weren't enough). There's a sense that "my spouse is not who I thought they were, my marriage is not what I thought it was, my *world* is not what I thought it was."

At the same time, there's the potential for using the insights/learnings from *any* crisis as an opportunity for growth—as reflected in the responses of the 18% who reported they had "actually grown in many ways." While no one would deliberately choose to go through this experience as a way to achieve personal growth, it is nevertheless possible to find some gain in the midst of such loss. This is reflective of the famous saying by Nietzsche: "That which doesn't kill me makes me stronger."

Re: Children:
(The next 2 questions were answered ONLY by those who had kids with spouse.)

What were the ages of the kids when you learned of the affair(s)? (721 Responses)

    48% - All under 6 years old

    25% - All between 6 and 13 years old

    27% - Various ages (including teenagers and grown kids)

Results: Two-thirds had children with spouse (perhaps related to fact that 76% are still married).

As indicated above, 721 of the 1,083 total respondents (or two-thirds) had kids with the spouse who had an affair. And in almost half those situations, the children were under 6 years old. This may be relevant to understanding the high percentage of respondents (76%) who reported they are still married and living together. While "staying together for the sake of the kids" is probably not as true today as in the past, it may still have a practical impact on decisions.

What did you tell the kids about the affair(s)? (710 Responses)

    28% - Didn't tell them

    32% - Told them, but only a very little

    40% - Told them most of the facts of the situation

Results: Reports of the degree of openness with children is higher than expected.

This is a surprising response – since one of the most consistent questions I've received through the years is the difficulty/dilemma of whether and what to tell the children. The above response would indicate that the 28% who "didn't tell them" may be related to those with children under the age of 6 and/or those who got a divorce.

My own sense of this issue is that most children know there's something wrong and are likely to imagine it has something to do with them. So they need to be given some kind of explanation for whatever emotional upheaval they may be seeing (or sensing) between their parents. Of course, each parent must make their own decisions about telling the children. (Personally, our children were 11 and 13 when we told them about my husband's affairs.)

Since children can best learn honesty by seeing it in their own families, "telling the children" may be seen as part of the larger responsibility of parents to prepare their children to cope with (or avoid) the difficulties inherent in any future intimate relationship. By teaching (and practicing) honesty with our children, we increase the chances that they will develop into sexually responsible adults and avoid the kind of deception inherent in having affairs.

Re: Staying Married:
(The next 2 questions were answered ONLY by those who stayed married.)

Has trust been rebuilt? (876 Responses)

   54% - No, still very guarded

   41% - Yes, but still somewhat cautious

   5% - Yes, secure in trustworthiness at this point

Results: Answering questions and fully discussing the situation is essential to rebuilding trust.

The chances for rebuilding trust depend on some basic behaviors on the part of the person who had an affair, including:
- being willing to answer your questions
- hanging in while you deal with the understandable emotions
- demonstrating a commitment to the relationship by severing contact with the other person

All this is aimed at strengthening the bond that has been broken. It demonstrates a willingness to handle problems in a responsible way instead of trying to bury them, avoid them, or hope they go away. There are no shortcuts; the only way through this situation is to face it head on and deal with it. Even then, it will be difficult for everyone.

The earlier section ("Statistical Analyses focusing on the Significance of Talking") provides evidence as to what's involved in rebuilding trust:
- Trust is more likely to be rebuilt when the spouse answers their questions.
- Trust is more likely to be rebuilt when they thoroughly discuss the whole situation.

Has the relationship "improved" compared to pre-affair days? (873 Responses)

25% - No, the relationship is more distant and strained

30% - Not actual improvement, but about the same as before

45% - Yes, it's better than before the affair(s)

Results: It's possible for a marriage to eventually be better than before the affair happened.

Most people assume that a marriage will inevitably be worse after it has been impacted by an affair. (And this is certainly true initially.) But the eventual state of the relationship depends on how the couple deal with the aftermath of the affair. The above response (indicating that 45% of the respondents say their relationship has "improved" compared to pre-affair days) may sound as if an affair might be an effective way to build a better marriage. Of course, that's nonsense. An affair is a crisis, pure and simple. It's what a couple does in response to the crisis that determines the future condition (or even future existence) of the marriage. Any improvement is *not* due to the affairs; it's due to the enormous amount of work a couple may undertake together to recover and rebuild following the affairs.

I can honestly say that I would never have chosen to go through all this in order to get to the kind of relationship we have now; but since it did happen, we learned from it and devoted ourselves to developing a strong bond based on complete honesty and a commitment to fairness and equality. Because of this, our trust is stronger than it ever was before the affairs. So there is hope that by actively working together, you can come through this with a stronger relationship and greater trust than before.

Re: Getting a Divorce:
(The next 3 questions were answered ONLY by those who got a divorce.)

Who initiated the divorce? (207 Responses)

58% - I did

30% - My spouse did

12% - It was a mutual decision

Results: Not all divorces are initiated by the hurt spouse.

The typical assumption is that a decision to divorce is made by the one who is hurt by their partner's affair, as represented by the 58% of respondents who initiated the divorce. In fact, those divorces that are specifically due to the impact of the affairs *are* likely to be represented by this group. But the 30% of divorces that are initiated by the spouses who had the affairs might have eventually happened anyway. Since it's quite rare for the spouse to divorce in order to marry the person with whom they had the affair, the divorces initiated by the spouses are not necessarily directly related to their affairs.

Of course, since there's a strong tradition of the "wife" being the one who actually "files" for the divorce (regardless of who primarily wishes the divorce), there's no clear way to interpret the meaning behind the responses. These results are simply a snapshot of "what happens" – not "why."

Have you been able to trust enough to develop another intimate relationship? (200 Responses)

41% - No, I'm very anxious about ever being vulnerable to being hurt again

35% - I've developed another relationship, but "hold back" somewhat

24% - I've developed a new "trusting" intimate relationship

Results: Affairs can have a long-term impact on ANY future relationship.

Ending the marriage doesn't end the impact of a spouse's affair on the ability to trust someone in a future relationship. In fact, "recovering" from a spouse's affair does not directly relate to staying married or getting a divorce. That's because *personal recovery* is separate from *recovering the marriage*.

Some people who stay married DO recover - and some DON'T.
Some people who get a divorce DO recover - and some DON'T.

Here are some keys steps involved in *personal recovery*:
- Accepting the fact that it happened (no more "if only..." or "why me?")
- Understanding the complex reasons for affairs (not *just* "personal failure").
- Deliberately focusing on dealing with it and talking openly about what happened.
- Allowing time to heal.
- Believing it's possible to recover.

Those who go through this process of personal recovery are the ones most likely to be able to trust enough to develop another intimate relationship. And since this process takes time, it's not surprising that only 24% of the respondents have been able to develop another relationship following their divorce.

What is the quality of any new relationship? (201 Responses)

39% - No new relationship

21% - Not as good as the early days of my previous marriage

40% - Better than any period of my previous marriage

Results: It is possible to form a good relationship with someone new in the future.

Despite initial misgivings about establishing new relationships following a divorce, twice as many of those who *do* go on to develop new relationships report that it is "better" than any period of the previous marriage as compared to "not as good as the early days of the previous marriage."

Re: Counseling:

The next 4 questions were answered ONLY by those who had therapy/counseling:

How many counselors did you see? (863 Responses)

27% - One

26% - Two

47% - Three or more

Results: Most people who sought counseling tried more than one counselor.

The fact that so many of the respondents (47%) saw "three or more" counselors is not absolute evidence of dissatisfaction with the first or second counseling efforts (since there may be additional reasons for seeking more than one counselor). However, the anecdotal evidence I have received through the years indicates that this is likely the case.

Here are a couple of typical comments:

"This is the third counselor we have tried, and I maintain a healthy skepticism; but she seems much better than the others."

"The first therapist told me in our second meeting (after my husband got up and walked out of the session) that I was 'weak and needy.' (I was in such shock!) The third therapist said at the end of our second meeting, "And next week, we will look at what you did to encourage this affair. (So my little world and brain became even more fried.)"

And here's an excerpt from *The Monogamy Myth* with another typical description:

> *"One woman told of going to a counselor who said (after two sessions) that her husband was 'sufficiently' guilt-ridden and sorry about what he'd done, and that if the marriage fell apart now, she could take the total blame for it as well as for ruining the rest of their kids' lives. She was so frustrated by this turn of events that she pleaded with her husband to go to a different counselor. Ironically, the second counselor continued the theme of placing 'blame,' this time determining that her husband was totally to blame and recommending that she get a divorce immediately. When she again became extremely distressed, the counselor suggested Valium for her nerves. By this time, she was too afraid to even try a third counselor. Unfortunately, this kind of difficult experience with counselors happens more often than it should, according to the many reports I received from BAN members."*

The responses to the next 3 questions were based ONLY on experience with "first" or "only" therapist/counselor:

Was the counselor helpful? (861 Responses)

57% - No, mostly frustrating

23% - Yes, but not as much as I'd like

20% - Yes, very helpful

Results: Most respondents did not find the counselor helpful.

These responses are some of the most striking in the survey. Over half (57%) reported that their experience (based on first or only therapist/counselor) was not helpful and mostly frustrating. These negative responses were not surprising since one of the consistent messages I have received through the years has been about a high level of frustration and dissatisfaction with counseling experiences.

A report of only 20% finding their counselor "very helpful" indicates an urgent need for therapists to more effectively deal with the issue of affairs. (See the "Advice from Respondents to Therapists," including the actual quotes of the participants, that follows this section.)

Did the counselor encourage honest communication about the affair(s)? (723 Responses)

23% - No, encouraged us to quickly cover highlights, then move on

45% - Yes, but on a limited time frame and to a limited degree

32% - Yes, very supportive of ongoing honest discussions

Results: The counselor plays a critical role in facilitating the process of honest communication.

It's encouraging that 32% reported that the counselor was "very supportive of ongoing honest discussions." This fits with the clear desires expressed by the respondents in overwhelmingly wanting a lot of information, including details about the affairs. As mentioned earlier, I have never seen any couple (even with the best effort and commitment to honesty) completely recover from the emotional impact of an affair in less than 2 years. So the fact that 45% reported that their counselor proposed "a limited time frame and to a limited degree" runs counter to the evidence reported earlier in the Statistical Analyses regarding the importance of honest communication in facilitating recovery and rebuilding the marriage.

Of course, another important aspect of facilitating the effort to "get answers" is to also focus on the impact of the hurt spouse's *reactions* to getting answers. Here's an excerpt from *The Monogamy Myth* that discusses the importance of reinforcing honesty in order for this process to continue:

> *"The ability to succeed in dealing honestly with an affair does not depend solely on the attitude and behavior of the one who had the affair. Their partner's reaction is critical because it serves either to reinforce honesty or to discourage it. Honesty about affairs comes in stages. First, there is the admission that it happened, then the many details that contribute to seeing the whole picture. A partner's reaction to the initial fact of the affair has a lot to do with the willingness of the person who had an affair to share any of the details.*
>
> *"A person who discovers their mate's affair usually feels justified in venting their feelings of hurt and anger. While they certainly have a right to those feelings, they need to recognize that punishing their mate for telling the truth will almost surely put an end to any further honesty. So while it may seem unfair, it's in their own best interest to try to reinforce whatever honesty is received if there is to be much hope for the honesty continuing.*
>
> *"This can be quite a challenge for the person who asks for honesty—to avoid punishing their partner for telling them what they want to know. It's understandable that a person feels badly about some of the information they receive, but this can be balanced by feeling good about their partner's honesty."*

Did the counselor focus directly on the issue of affairs? (725 Responses)

59% - No, mainly focused on general marital problems

28% - Yes, but not as strongly or clearly as I'd like

13% - Yes, very directly dealt with this issue

Results: Very few counselors deal directly with the issue of affairs.

Responses to the 35 Multiple-Choice Questions

Only 13% reported that their counselors "very directly dealt with this issue." But 28% reported that the focus on affairs was "not as strongly or clearly as I'd like," and over half (59%) reported that their counselors focused "mainly on general marital problems. This appears to be one of the specific reasons for the "mostly frustrating" experiences with counseling.

One of the main drawbacks to using typical marital therapy when dealing with affairs is that focusing on the marriage (and specifically whatever problems exist in the marriage) inadvertently reinforces the idea that the affair was *caused* by the marital problems or by a failure to "meet your partner's needs." Suggesting that an affair is due to "unmet needs" implies that the hurt partner is to "blame" when their spouse has an affair—and is responsible for keeping it from happening again.

It's easy (after the fact) to identify the specific problems in any particular marriage and then assign a "cause and effect"—as if the identified problems caused the affair. However, since *all* marriages have problems, if those particular problems hadn't existed, there would have been some *other* problems—and *those* would have been identified as the cause of the affair.

While marital problems or unmet needs may be part of one set of factors that contribute to affairs, the *reason* is far more complex than this one simple explanation. In fact, affairs are due to a combination of three different *sets* of factors: 1) factors that "push" people into affairs (including marital problems or unmet needs), 2) factors that "pull" people into affairs (novelty, curiosity, excitement, etc.) and 3) societal factors (secrecy, fascination/glorification of affairs, etc.) These factors are more thoroughly explored in *The Monogamy Myth*).

Of course, even this expanded understanding of the combination of factors that contribute to affairs is still limited in that *all* the factors together only explain why someone might *want* to have an affair. The "trump card" (that is necessary in order for someone to *act* on the desire) is a willingness to deceive their partner. So if there is such a thing as *one* reason for affairs, it would be this willingness to be dishonest and deceptive—not the easy "excuse" that the affair was caused by marital problems. (There are many options for dealing with marital problems, and having an affair is the least legitimate of all.)

When so many counselors (59% of those referred to in this study) "mainly focused on general marital problems," it's not surprising that most people see counseling for affairs as not being very helpful. In fact, little has changed during the years between the initial publication of *The Monogamy Myth* and the time of this survey.

Help for Therapists

Here's an excerpt from *The Monogamy Myth*:

"The standard advice of counselors, therapists...has been for couples to examine themselves and the conditions within their relationship to determine why an affair happened.

"Since most people in the helping professions have their training or orientation in terms of psychology rather than sociology, they tend to see things in terms of personal, individual problems. They bring this bias to their work with couples dealing with affairs, and this personal orientation reinforces the attitude that affairs are due exclusively to individual weaknesses. This approach is considered to be the appropriate one when couples are in counseling, as illustrated by the following description of the role of a counselor.

'A good marriage counselor will help a couple talk about the reasons for cheating in terms of the marriage and about the problems that lead a partner to seek an extramarital relationship. In counseling, the couple discuss what they feel the marriage lacks or where the rough spots are, and then with the counselor's help they work to correct their problems.'

"Almost any book, magazine, or newspaper advice column dealing with this issue reinforces this view of affairs as caused only by problems in the relationship. Following are some typical examples:

'Cheating always points to a weakness in your relationship.'

'Ask yourself why you need to go outside the marriage, what is lacking in your relationship.'

'Affairs are then attempts to meet important needs that are unmet within the context of the marriage.'

"The tendency of the experts to focus almost exclusively on personal failure and inadequacies strongly reinforces the personal view of affairs. And this interpretation contributes to the difficulty of being able to fully recover from the emotional impact of this experience. Despite the fact that 85 percent of the members of BAN had sought some kind of counseling, many expressed disappointment with the help they had received. Most of them continued to struggle with unresolved feelings for many years following their experience."

One Person's Story of their Experience with Counseling

(Unfortunately, this is typical of stories I have heard through the years.)

August 1999 I confront my wife of 18 years about her extramarital affair. She confirms that she has become emotionally attached with someone that she works with but insists that "nothing happened." I am unconvinced. Over the following three years, we see three marriage counselors.

The first counselor is a psychotherapist. His training is in the psychoanalysis of individuals. I doubt he has any specific clinical training in marital therapy. I describe our marriage problems to him and he asks my wife if she has (in fact) had a sexual affair and she denies it. He becomes very angry with me when my wife reveals that I have been reading "The Monogamy Myth" (a very good book about recovering from extramarital affairs). He tells me that I am being insensitive and cruel to read a book about affairs in front of my wife and he implies that I am attempting to punish her. He suggests that (if I must read a book of that kind) I should do so in private.

At our sixth or seventh (and final) session (after talking primarily about improved communication techniques), I reveal that I am frustrated because I believe that my wife has had a full-blown affair which she has not told the truth about. I explain carefully why I do not believe my wife, describing some of the ways that she appears avoidant, evasive, and deceptive. At this point, the therapist becomes visibly angry and tells me that if I do not trust my wife then I have no choice but to divorce. He talks for 10 or 15 minutes about technical issues in psychotherapy. The gist of it was that in therapy, he MUST assume that the things that his clients tell him MUST be true, otherwise the "psychodynamics are all wrong." I still don't know what that means.

We work with our second therapist for more than a dozen sessions on learning to do things for each other that will help to increase mutual affection. We talk about gender differences and various factors (children, jobs, etc.) that can help to increase the distance between partners in a long term relationship. Finally, I ask directly whether we will be discussing my wife's "non-affair." The therapist advises against that, explaining that he feels that my wife is "too vulnerable."

Our third therapist believes that affairs are merely symptoms of underlying marriage problems and works to correct those. For 15 to 20 sessions, our focus is on family of origin issues, particularly problems with things like our narcissistic parents. Finally, I again describe some of the ways that my wife appears avoidant, evasive, and deceptive. However, this therapist, like the first, believes that the things that her clients tell her must be true.

June 2002. My wife reveals that she has, in fact, had a full-blown, sordid, romantic love affair which was continuing while we were seeing our first therapist.

Help for Therapists

I feel betrayed not only by my wife but also by the three marriage counselors that we have seen over the past three years. Re-reading "The Monogamy Myth" now, I find that the author, Peggy Vaughan, discusses this problem in her book in depth. (That happens to me a lot, by the way, to re-read "The Monogamy Myth" and some other self help books and find things that I hadn't remembered reading the first time).

I believe now that marriage counselors either support honesty or they do not. The middle ground is rife with pitfalls. When a person has an affair, they become dishonest. It is universal. It is true by definition. After an affair, people continue to be dishonest. That is also universal. The exceptions are exceedingly rare. Marriage counselors should know this and they should respond accordingly. At least 50% of the couples that they counsel are there because one of the partners has had an affair. Affairs are their bread and butter.

Therapists spend much of their time encouraging clients to take responsibility for their own actions except when it comes to having affairs. Their silence on the subject of affairs implies that affairs are not important. Our third counselor paid lip service to the idea that my wife should take responsibility for her "non-affair" but the therapist also was clear that the affair was not the problem. "It is only a symptom" was her mantra. Affairs don't cause problems in marriages. Problems in marriages cause affairs. It is almost impossible to imagine that the cause-effect arrow would point in only one direction in the case of any other marital or individual problem.

Marital therapists often try to teach couples how to communicate honestly and openly except when it comes to having affairs. I cannot imagine another problem that a marriage counselor would advise, even insist, that a couple avoid talking about. What marriage counselor would advise that someone ignore a partner's pedophilia, to put it in the past, and to focus on the present and future? People are not "too vulnerable" to talk about affairs. They are "too vulnerable" not to.

Of course there are good, conscientious therapists who do a lot of good. Of course marital therapy is hard, emotionally draining work. Of course, there are always going to be some real idiots practicing marital therapy. I can understand how difficult it must be to sit in a room with a couple in a long-term relationship when one of them has been having an affair. I don't expect therapists to leave their doubts and fears about themselves and their own marriages outside the door when they step into their office. I can also understand the therapeutic advantage of declaring that everyone always tells the truth in therapy. I can understand how difficult it would make therapy if the therapist must continually assess the truthfulness of their clients. But having an affair is dumb. Lying about it is dumber. But assuming that an unfaithful partner is always going to be truthful is the dumbest thing I have ever heard and it could be dangerous.

The assumption that someone is "too vulnerable" to talk about their affair is insulting and diminishing. Mostly, it insults and diminishes an unfaithful partner. People who have affairs don't suddenly become children who need to be protected from themselves. People who have affairs need to take responsibility for themselves, not only to help their partners recover, help rebuild their marriage, or lay the groundwork for a better divorce, but also for their own personal development. In no other area is it imaginable that a therapist would encourage a client to move on without dealing with a royal mess that the client themself has created.

As Frank Pittman says, "Honestly, it is safe to talk openly about affairs. It saves lives and marriages to do so." There is a big problem out there that needs to be addressed. Sometimes I think that people like Peggy Vaughan, Frank Pittman, and Shirley Glass are just voices from the wilderness. It seems to me that marital therapists need some clinical training in talking to clients about their affairs. Yes, it will probably be hard but I believe that it can be done. Perhaps professional organizations need to hear more often from the casualties of ignorance.

Invitation to Submit Names of Effective Therapists/Counselors

In order to help people locate a therapist or counselor (in their area) who is effective in dealing directly with affairs, I invite the submission of names to be included on a list posted on my Website.

So if you personally know a therapist or counselor whose approach fits with what people are seeking (as reflected in the following "Advice" from respondents to the survey), please go to Peggy's Website and fill out the form for recommending a therapist.

Website address: www.dearpeggy.com

Advice from Respondents' in Responses to the Question:

"How could therapists be more effective in dealing with affairs?"

In order to determine what would promote more successful experiences with counseling, respondents to the Questionnaire were invited to contribute (on an open-ended basis) whatever Comments ("Advice") they would like to pass along to therapists to help them be more effective in dealing with affairs. The responses were sorted according to similar points. Following each of the points listed are the "Direct Quotes of Comments by Respondents" that led to identifying each of the major points.

1. Deal directly with the affair, not just ordinary marriage counseling.

2. Deal with the emotional impact of the affair.

3. Don't "blame" the affair on the hurt spouse.

4. Be supportive of those couples who want to try to save the marriage.

5. Don't keep secrets or too quickly believe lies of the one who had an affair.

6. See both parties together.

7. Be aware of the impact of your gender/beliefs/experience on therapy.

8. Don't expect the hurt party to forget the affair or "set it aside and go on."

9. Help clients connect with others who have "been there."

10. Be well-informed about affairs and provide good information.

11. Encourage honest communication and answering all questions.

12. Miscellaneous Comments about Therapists

Following are the direct quotes for each of the above points—as they were submitted:

1. Deal directly with the affair, not just ordinary marriage counseling.

Direct Quotes of Comments by Respondents:

Our therapist doesn't seem to think we will profit by discussing the affair directly, rather would prefer to just work on other issues between us. I feel the affair is the single biggest issue between us, and we should be discussing this much more in depth, and directly dealing with the affair. Our affair was years in the past when he finally admitted it to me, and the therapist seems to think it is "too far back" to work on. But how else will I get over this?

It is ridiculous to think that soon after an affair is discovered and the couple is in therapy that any work on the marriage can occur right away. The only focus should be on surviving the emotional turmoil by helping the couple discuss the affair; not the marriage, but the affair.

Counselors need to focus more on the actual problem of adulterous affairs...I received very little counseling on what caused that particular problem and how to deal with it....too much generalization about just ordinary marriage counseling...

Don't gloss over or dance around the issues. Deal with it head on and give some guidance as to what can be expected when in the healing process, and work toward success.

Therapists needs to deal directly with the affair - not just general marital problems. Our marriage was in trouble prior to the affair. So he sees it as we "both" were wrong, so let's just forget it and go on. I see a tremendous difference in marriage problems and sleeping with someone. Blameshifting. I desperately needed to talk about it and he pretty much refused. As a result, we have been living as "roommates" since it happened. I immediately accepted blame for my part of our marriage problems and forgave him for the affair, but he couldn't forgive me. So I grew bitter about the fact that he couldn't forgive me or couldn't respond to me at all. After a year and a half, he is ready to move on and I am stuck in this bitter state. As a result, we are presently talking about divorce so we can at least move in some direction. I think if the therapist had encouraged us to talk about it instead of just "deal with prior marriage problems and move on," we would have been able to work through it. It was an "out" for him, because he didn't want to talk about it, and for me I still see that as something he shares with her and I am not a part of.

Our counselor focused on other events and "losses" in my life, rather than helping to deal with the affair and my reaction to it in particular. I entered a depression, and the counselor was no help in dealing with this at all. Perhaps I was overly optimistic about what a counselor could do. Also, he was provided through a work support agreement, so perhaps he was just putting in his six sessions rather than looking towards actually helping me cope. I found my personal study of more value than the counseling. There may also be a timing element on the counseling. This occurred very early, so I don't think that he could have been very helpful in the healing, which couldn't have occurred until later. Perhaps it would have been more helpful if he could have described what I had to go through before healing was possible. The counseling didn't really help either of us.

I am a trained psychologist, familiar with personal relationship research and counseling myself, and I only now realize how little professional counselors and even marital therapists know about affairs and how to deal with them. Like friends and relatives, professional helpers essentially seem to base their interventions on stereotypes, generalizations and folk wisdom about affairs, rather than on sound research. It is extremely painful if your partner had (or has) an affair to be confronted with the axiom that "something must have been wrong with the spouse or with the relationship" to explain the affair happening. It is like blaming a rape victim for having seduced the rapist, and it feels very wrong. Dealing with the affair of a spouse is a traumatic event, and clinically is very comparable to a post-traumatic stress disorder. Professional help would probably be much more effective if counselors would deal with the issue as a trauma and draw on the literature on the treatment of PTSD, rather than to systematically regard affairs as signs of underlying relational problems.

I believe strongly that it is inappropriate for a therapist or counselor to tell a couple to move past the affair issue and on to the general problems in the marriage before thoroughly discussing the affair.

Do not treat the affair the same as other marital problems. It overshadows issues of communication or division of work in the home. To treat it as just one of many problems is insensitive and insulting. This is a grief process, at least two years long.

Although the therapist listened to me, she made no comments about how I felt. She focused only on changes I should make for myself. It was as if she were telling me to forget everything and concentrate on building a life for myself. I realize that rebuilding self-esteem is important but so is helping someone in my position to understand that what they're experiencing is normal. I felt that there was something very wrong with me because I wasn't angry with my husband and didn't want revenge. I wanted honest discussion and to understand why it had happened. I've yet to feel vengeful.

The counselor mostly focused on me and how I could continue with my life. I am a good "talker." I am smart and know what the right thing to do is, whether I can really deal with it is another matter. He decided I was fine, and said to call him whenever I felt I needed help. Of course, I never made another appointment.

Since infidelity is very common in marital difficulties, it should be discussed openly, even if it is difficult. In my case, one reason it wasn't discussed, is because my husband would have walked out of the therapy, because he felt his "spiritual friend" had nothing to do with our troubles. SO to keep him "in therapy" and comfortable, it wasn't discussed. Instead we nit-picked at other issues, that were never a problem, until he decided to re-create and rewrite our 26 year marriage, and make it all negative. So issues were brought up that had never been issues. But he made them sound so bad... all to justify his going outside of the marriage and breaking our trust bond. He linked his "going to his spiritual friend" to a desperate, drowning situation.... as if he was such a victim of misery, that he had no choice. It has all been very confusing and convoluted. I think therapists should establish what the clients are trying to hide immediately... and deal with why they are doing it. No therapist had the guts to be straight with my husband. They were too afraid to lose him, and I was too.

The counselor after the first affair saw me alone once and then attempted marital counseling. I feel this was a mistake.

I went to two marriage counseling sessions with my husband (my idea). The first session we didn't even mention the affair. The second one was only about the affair. After that, my husband continued with the therapist on a spotty basis, and I had left the area (and state) and found another therapist for myself.

My husband had the affair. We went to marriage counseling (about 3 months) even though he hasn't totally ended the affair and doesn't know if he wants to save the marriage. Our therapist wanted to concentrate on the problems in the marriage that led to the affair and I wanted to concentrate on the affair for which I am totally consumed.

Our counselor was trained in family systems and most of the time was spent on family of origin, etc. While I think this was helpful, I expected more discussion on the affair, which was still ongoing. I have suffered a major depression over the last year and am still in personal therapy. My husband and I are currently legally separated, which I instigated due to "not being able to take it any more."

Our counselor's philosophy was unhelpful. She was very uncomfortable with me talking about the affairs of my husband during the times I saw her alone, as she did not want to be privy to information that had not come up in a couple's setting. Yet, when we had couple's therapy, my husband did not want to talk about the affairs, or lied about them, and/or denied them. So we could not discuss them in the couple's setting. At home, my husband would not discuss the affairs or lied about them. I gave therapy a good try, for about 9 months after I learned of the affairs, but finally opted out of it, as I saw no benefit to me. My husband said that he was going to continue to attend himself, but he did not. I think a more skilled counselor might have made a difference.

2. Deal with the emotional impact of the affair.

Direct Quotes of Comments by Respondents:

Deal with the pain, sense of loss, sense of aloneness, overwhelming sense of disillusionment. In other words, first-aid and damage-control first, please. Therapists need to look for it: the damage, the personal trauma; it may not be apparent.

I was suicidal and put in the hospital, totally worthless. I felt worse than when I went in. After being betrayed by my husband, I was treated like a prisoner with no rights. Counselor was very uncaring and rough. I needed to know I would survive this great pain.

I needed immediate help on the healing of the pain inflicted upon me. Every counselor or therapist I visited started with the basics of my early childhood and why something like this would hurt me. I became very frustrated during the whole experience of therapy and finally stopped after 1 year.

I feel our counselor is on my husband's side; she hasn't offered or told my husband to hold on to me when I feel bad or cry. He has left the house to get away to deal with it, and to let me think about it. I feel he is just running away. When I cry he says I just want sympathy; I feel betrayed by the only person I thought I loved and loved me too. She wants to see me alone to help me deal with the situation. Well I feel she should also tell him how to help me feel wanted and loved again if he really wants to stay with me. We are the victims here but we're the ones that need help? Something sounds wrong with that to me. I'm the one that's hurting and need love, not therapy. Just help to deal with the feelings of betrayal and feeling unloved, that another younger girl took away from me.

A counselor should try to help talk through the pain and let the faithful spouse realize he/she is not the only one going through this pain. It doesn't help that person but at least there is reassurance that they are not alone. I think at this same time, the counselor should make the unfaithful spouse knowledgeable about what kind of emotions follow this type of pain. I know that personally, I initially felt almost a sort of relief to know that I was not "crazy" for having those instinctive feelings for four years. My husband did nothing to make me feel otherwise. I was so glad when he finally admitted to me that this happened. He did it out of fear that the other woman would tell me first. (I got an interesting phone call a week prior to his admission.) Next, I felt like someone had literally sucked out my insides and cried like I never have in my life. Then, the anger started. I wanted to kill him for doing that to me. Then, I wanted him so badly that our sex life became better than it has EVER been since we've been together. After the sex, boom, back to the old feelings of insecurity, no self-esteem, doubt that he is still with this person, etc. I have really learned to take it day by day and get away by myself when those feelings begin.

Really wish my therapist had focused on how to deal with lingering anger and hurt! He focused more on my personal growth, but I needed help with the marriage more at the time.

Just having someone to listen to was great. It was nice to be able to talk with a professional who did not care if I cried, got angry, or just wanted to "chat" about everything else but the affair. My therapist was excellent and I felt that he really was able to assist me to put the entire experience in perspective.

3. Don't "blame" the affair on the hurt spouse.

Direct Quotes of Comments by Respondents:

I think it is very important to let a spouse who is cheated on know that it is NOT his or her "fault." While I blame myself for taking his abuse, I do not blame myself for his breaking his vow to me.

Therapists need to teach the person who had the affair to take responsibility for their actions and to not find the blame in the other partner. There are always options within a relationship and hurting the one you love should not be an option to express dissatisfaction within the marriage.

DO NOT try to find what the offended party did to CONTRIBUTE to his/her partner's decision to have an affair. This is misdirecting responsibility.

I am furious that some would say it is the wife's fault for not meeting his needs. He did not want me to meet his needs! I tried everything to stop it! He was on a project in another state and I would drive to go spend time with him on weekends and be available for his call. I kept physically fit; there was no excuse for that part. And now I don't have any desire for him to meet mine! We are on our last leg, married for 20 years! He indicated that it would never have happened if I had only been able to live with him = my fault! Now, he is away on another project, the first we have been apart since his affair....and we all know what he's up to! What a mess, what a joke, what a life! And we have the label of the "conservative Christian family"! What a JOKE!!!!

Therapists shouldn't tell the offended spouse that the affair is "just a symptom" of underlying marital problems. That doesn't help alleviate the hurt or address the sense of betrayal. It also gives the spouse having the affair a convenient "tag line" to hide behind in order to avoid dealing with the issue in a forthright, honest way. Saying "it's just a symptom" also can tend to make the aggrieved spouse feel like it is their fault somehow. Let's be very clear--having an affair is a deliberate, conscious choice, and the pain inflicted should not be minimized or excused.

I think it would have been good for my therapist to focus on my guilt feelings that I could have prevented his behavior. I still feel responsible and that my actions caused it to happen. He admits that it was his choice to have an affair, but in the same sentence he would say that I wasn't always there for him. But, when there are children involved, it makes you try much harder to repair what you can. And I am, for now.

I think the hardest part of therapy was that the therapist kept seeing the affair as a "symptom" of the marriage disease, when actually the marriage was pretty strong before the affair. The therapist kept wanting to make it "equal blame" I guess so as not to scare off my spouse, but that led to him actually equating my less-than-perfect housekeeping with the spouse's adultery. He did however correctly diagnose depression as a problem with my husband, but didn't even suggest that that might be the cause of the discontent that made him hate our marriage. (It was only reading some books about affairs that I felt I was right to be angry, that I was right to think my husband had crossed the line, and that his behavior was his own fault, not mine.) I needed to hear that nothing I did "made" him have the affair, and I never heard that from the therapist (who, by the way, worked at a church-based counseling service). He seemed far more interested in my minor sins than my husband's major sins... and I don't know why. I think it also let my husband off the hook--it took YEARS before he took responsibility for his actions, and he often used the therapist's words to "prove" that if I'd been a perfect wife, he'd never have had to stray. What I needed to hear was that even an imperfect wife (which is to say all wives) deserves commitment and honesty. We did a bit of "therapist-shopping" and I did find a counselor who didn't placate my husband, and told me over and over that his actions were his doing, not mine, but of course he never heard that).

Need to help the wronged person believe it was not their fault and to help them get through the pain.

My husband lied to me several times about not having an affair. But 3-5 years later finally admitted to one. He's never had remorse and acts as though the whole ordeal is my problem to deal with. He is considered mentally healthy because he does not allow others to influence his life and what he wants! I'm the one with the problem because I have allowed him to influence me. So some counselors have said.

The counselors I went to were very kind and tried to help. What they may not have known was that I was hoping for a magic formula to save my marriage. It may be helpful if they knew that those in my position are looking for this and help them understand that another person's behavior is beyond your control.

We've been in counseling for over a year, and I have learned through counseling that I was never the problem, but that my husband was and still is going through a mid-life crisis and some identity issues. Counseling has helped me to grow as person and rebuild some of my lost self-esteem.

He has been seeing this therapist for almost a year and I believe she is doing more damage to our marriage. It doesn't take a degree to figure out that trusting someone is what this is all about. I asked him if he discussed what happened with her and he did. I cannot believe she turned this around and made me the bad guy. It seems he now believes that the affair is over and I should trust simply because he says so!! He came home after his session angrier then when he left. What else did she tell him?

Have the guts to tell the cheater they DO have a problem and it's up to them to get some help or to go ahead and leave the betrayed till they get some help. I felt it wasn't fair to infer that I could have contributed in some way. I felt right up front the therapist should have said NONE of his behavior had anything to do with me, because it did not.

I think the most effective thing is getting the person having the affair to take responsibility for that particular action. There are lots of reasons for having an affair, however, under similar circumstances there are a variety of responses—of which an affair is only ONE CHOICE. The choice to have an affair rather than divorcing, taking up a hobby, etc., indicates a lack of commitment and basic integrity and the person initiating this action needs to take FULL responsibility for their actions and not try to blame that choice on the spouse. Additionally, it is my feeling that this is the only way that things can heal. If the "offending" spouse cannot take responsibility for his/her own actions, then trying to work things out becomes a mute point since they will be unable to take the steps needed to right the situation through their own responsible actions (the victim syndrome).

My therapist won't explore "why" my husband had an affair. She says sometimes there isn't an answer to that question. I don't believe that. If a person won't explore what got them to the point of having an affair (they don't "just happen"), then that person won't grow, the marital relationship won't grow and the spouse is left feeling like it's all their fault because they must have done something wrong.

4. Be supportive of those couples who want to try to save the marriage.

Direct Quotes of Comments by Respondents:

Therapists need to encourage working to rebuild the marriage. I have a fear of going for more therapy as I'm afraid it will cause my marriage to end and I don't want that. My husband is not very cooperative at this point in rebuilding our marriage.

We are currently in therapy to make a decision about whether to divorce or stay married. I have not been able to totally commit to the relationship even though we have still been married for 7 years after the affair. My spouse has been very patient with me. I don't think our marriage therapy helped except to get us through the pain of the first few months. Nothing was resolved or discussed as to how we would change or proceed from there.

One thing I did appreciate was that all the counselors we saw honored our attempt to rebuild the marriage and didn't ever suggest divorce, though one said our chances of survival were slim.

My husband had been in counseling for another problem, and I called and talked to the counselor. He helped give me tremendous hope that the affair did not mean the end of my marriage by basically profiling my husband. He gave me hope that my husband was not the only person to do this, and that there are reasons beyond our marital relationship, which was very good. Many people asked him "Were you guys having trouble," he told me he answered them no. He had major self-esteem problems.

We were very committed as a couple to stay married and work through our difficulties. We have continued to do work, and re-committed individually to our relationship. I am not afraid to address sensitive issues and dialog about them. We operated more in avoidance before the affair. We do not do that now. I believe our marriage got stronger.

Eventually my husband and I worked things out and he returned but I don't feel the therapist had anything to do with bringing that about. I usually felt worse after a session with her than before it, as if my desire for reconciliation was foolish and shortsighted. I later found another therapist (after my husband returned) and what I received from her in terms of rebuilding my self-worth has been beneficial. But sorting out all the ramifications of my husband's affair has been done by following my gut feelings.

My counselor kept pushing me to make a decision about the marriage. I had told him in the beginning that I was going to give it a year before I made a decision. My world had totally changed and I wasn't going to make a decision based on anger or humiliation without having tried to figure out what happened.

My husband lied to the counselors (we'd switch since he didn't like their approach). In turn (since they knew both sides and I was in the dark a lot) they would ask me why I was still in the marriage and try to encourage me to be strong enough to get out.

The counselor has done a wonderful job helping me individually--to set boundaries, to go through the grieving process, and to re-define myself after this most hideous (but growth-producing) journey. While I realize I was/am seeking individual counseling to help with my individual issues leading up to and coping with my husband's affair, there have been many times I've felt shortchanged or that my feelings have been sort of "dismissed." By that I mean negating certain choices I've made as unhealthy for me and therefore not worthy of consideration. At the present time I have chosen to stay in my marriage, primarily because of my children (6 and 12) and our family life as a whole. I vehemently feel divorce AT THIS TIME would completely undo my son (age 6). My husband is still quite self-involved at this point and isn't investing much energy in putting the relationship back together. This is the catch, and my counselor thinks it is in my best interest to cut my losses and move on. I agree with him with regard to myself personally, but am unwilling to put my children through that emotional ordeal, at least at this point in time. I would appreciate my counselor's acknowledging this place that I'm in and seeing the bigger picture of me and perhaps focusing on ways to grow individually within and in spite of a less-than-perfect marriage, rather than simply dismissing staying in the marriage as "not an option." I feel completely invalidated and insignificant when I express my desire to try to stay together "for the sake of the children" and with the hope that our marriage could improve because of this. Twenty years and 2 children's security is a lot to cast away.

The therapist missed addressing several points about the affair(s). He acted as if our marriage was over and didn't pick up on my husband's (then) ambivalence.

Neither of our therapists gave us any practical trust or relationship rebuilding "exercise" suggestions or many practical ideas. We have had to stumble on our own through different ideas.

We went to counseling soon after the affair was found out. This was extremely helpful in my getting a better perspective on what she did and what was happening. We had about thirteen sessions. About two thirds were individual (split between my wife and me) and the rest (four sessions I think) were together. I have developed an admiration for the counseling profession which I didn't have before. This was my wife's and my only experience with counseling. Without counseling my decision to try to rebuild our marriage may have been abandoned.

The therapist focuses on me, not my husband or the marital problems. Though I told her I did not feel I wanted to end the marriage, she is still asking me if I need to leave the marriage. I really need help rebuilding, not leaving! I need help to fully forgive, not wonder if I can make it. I already know I can make it and I know how to pack. My husband has a problem, and I do not feel I can abandon him if he is working to correct this, and he is trying. It would be most helpful if counselors would embrace healing and focus on repair rather than on personal issues of my own development! What we need is help to repair, but that seems to be available only through books and the net!

5. Don't keep secrets or too quickly believe lies of the one who had an affair.

Direct Quotes of Comments by Respondents:

First counselor knew that my husband was still having affair. He let us go there for 8 months and never let me know that. I feel he should have told me somehow.

My ex-husband never acknowledged having the affairs, even though he was "caught." The therapist believed him, and would never delve into the problem. There was no closure.

I would strongly urge the counselor to pay attention to the "victim's" need to deal with the whole truth, and that the truth be obtained from the responsible party. My husband continued to lie through three years of counseling and much blaming of me because I did not believe his stories and untruths. It finally came out that he was indeed still lying about duration, frequency, other affairs, etc. Meanwhile, all efforts at my trying to repair etc., were thwarted.

In my situation, it has been over 3 months and my spouse has yet to disclose the affair happened. This will ultimately force me to proceed with divorce as I am now finding that the deception is almost harder to handle than the physical reality of the affair itself. It would be helpful for counselors to be able to outline a hard-line plan of action or strategy for this scenario.

Therapists need to try to force honesty. My husband's disclosures about his infidelities surfaced haltingly over an 8-month period due to constant pressure from me. No counselor addressed the issue. Swallowing a bitter pill is better than having one measured out to you over a period of time.

My therapist and my husband decided I didn't need to know…that I wasn't strong enough to handle the information. It was an absurd assumption, particularly because I kept asking if an affair was going on directly to my husband and the therapist (who knew). The counseling prior to my investigating on my own and "discovering" the affair was a farce. I kept saying something is not right here are you having an affair...none of what is happening makes any sense. I kept saying in the counseling sessions...I don't understand why you are pulling away from me, all I want is a slice of your life for me and the kids. In retrospect I was so rational and so confused because my common sense approach was going nowhere. Of course once I discovered the affair it all made sense...my husband wasn't rational at all; how could he be, he was so busy blaming me and trying to make himself feel okay about himself that rational thought wasn't even able to enter the picture. What was particularly frustrating is that our therapist told my husband not to tell because it would most likely end the marriage. Actually it was the continuation of the dishonesty and my husband 's inability to face up to what he had done that almost ended the marriage. No solid worthwhile relationship can be built or maintained on a foundation of secrecy or lies...honesty must be the foundation.

Our first visit to the therapist was at a crisis point. It occurred when my husband came back to see me after he'd left to go to the other woman and I discovered her existence. We were interviewed separately and I've no idea what he told her. A few days after the visit my husband returned to the
other woman and I was left to the therapist.

I think the therapist should enforce honesty. And have a personality test on him and maybe me.

I think therapists we saw did a fine job in handling our marital issues. I don't feel it was any failure on their part that brought about the end of our marriage. I believe there are people out there that simply can't be helped, due to their complete lack of admitting their part in the marital problems. In my case, my ex-husband had genuine and severe mental problems. I think that went unrecognized in all the therapies we received but one. He was very good at covering things up. I think if I could say anything to contribute, it would be that if the therapist has any kind of "red flag" waving, pay attention to that, trust their instincts about someone. And sometimes its necessary to break that confidentiality code to save a life.

I suspect that my therapist (who was great) knew something was going on with my husband (he was not as forthcoming with issues as I was) and I wish that she would have INSISTED that he see her privately. I certainly am not blaming her; he was the idiot, and still refuses to come clean, and maybe I should just forget about the whole marriage and get rid of him. He refuses to continue with counseling, and I feel that it is one of the only ways we will ever be able to communicate honestly again.

When my husband and I went to a marriage counselor it was not confirmed he was having an affair. All of our sessions were about problems within the marriage and it was not effective because my husband was not being completely honest and could not admit to his affairs.

I know that after a year of counseling things are much better than they were before it happened. I still have a hard time believing the things I hear from my mate and I know in my heart that it's wrong to feel that way, but sometimes I just can't help it. We love each other very much and I know he cares what happens or he wouldn't be still going to counseling, but it still hurts.

My husband went to counseling and told his therapist about the affair without my knowing about it. (I attended a few sessions.) After I found out, I would not go because I feel that having me sit there discussing my problems meeting my husbands "needs" (all the while his therapist and he were aware that someone else was meeting them) was dishonest and unfair. It has made me believe that persons who take money to provide these services may not be as ethical as they profess.

6. See both parties together.

Direct Quotes of Comments by Respondents:

I wish that couples would go together to counseling, instead of just the one. If both don't go, there's little hope in resolving all issues. One or two sessions with the spouse isn't enough. I wish that the spouse would continue going to therapy with the other spouse--to help each other and to make them feel the pain that you're going through without always being in denial.

My husband and I had separate counselors (their suggestion) that set up a "them" against "us" scenario. I think we would have made better progress using the same counselor.

When my husband and I first started counseling we were on the verge of divorce. We had talked the subject to death and couldn't get past it. The counselor suggested we stop talking about it. We agreed and that saved our marriage, I believe. BUT! She then saw my husband alone to treat his depression and we never went back together to solve anything. I felt very left out and hurt, like I was the one who got run over and the driver of the car got all the help, attention and healing. So it has been months of working on him and not a word from the counselor about how I might be doing. She made a big mistake by not coming back to the marriage and asking how we both were doing. In many ways our marriage is better but I am definitely not healed.

We have found it very helpful to both have individual and marriage counseling with the same therapist. I know some advise against, but we feel it helps for the therapist to see all sides and to see how we act together and separate.

The only way that any counselor/therapist will help is if the spouse went to therapy as well. A one-on-one, then both in the same room discussing it, without the spouse walking out and not returning.

My husband left immediately, and has refused to tell me about the affair nor confront me about any issues, including our child together. I have been seeing the marriage counselor by myself and still in the process of a divorce, even though I am not ready for the divorce yet.

The counselor I went to didn't work on the problem at all. Discussed where to go and my feelings. No joint discussions. Same counselor for both of us.

One note about therapy, most of the sessions have been between my wife and the therapist. She has been tentatively diagnosed with a sexual addiction. They are working on that and other issues first. When those have been resolved, we will start (I hope) to begin to deal with the marriage.

7. Be aware of the impact of your gender/beliefs/experience on therapy.

Direct Quotes of Comments by Respondents:

My female therapist was more open and understanding of my feelings/reactions of anger regarding the affair. The male therapist I saw was more of the thinking, leave the past in the past and move on. She was more sympathetic than he was.

Both therapists I met with seemed to gloss over the anger and rage. One told me to scream in the car with the doors and windows shut (helpful at times), the other pretty much ignored it. I felt like a walking nerve--so angry, hurt, scared--and the people who I wanted to help me, i.e. the therapists (both men, I am a woman) had no real grasp of the pain. I would like to meet with a woman next. Maybe they did the right thing, I do not really know, but it sure felt like a big part of my experience was not being understood or dealt with.

I think it helps more if the therapist has been in your shoes.

Help for Therapists

I believe every single counselor, therapist, author brings to the table their own history and rationalizations to the issues of infidelity. Until the gamesmanship of how infidelity is currently viewed or rationalized etc., there are no reasons to stop the behavior of people who are simply out of order, period.

The therapist was rather judgmental I thought and pretty hard on my husband. I think his forcefulness ("No contact with the other woman," which was very strong) put my husband on the defensive. I agreed with the therapist but his delivery to my husband was very aggressive. I learned later from a friend that had recommended him to me for our couple counseling, that this therapist's wife had cheated on him and been a liar and left him for someone else several years ago. This man was a very good therapist but I think his own experience compromised his neutrality. He told me in a private session that my husband was a cheat and a liar--trying to talk me out of reaching out to him when I found he had cheated on me again. Therapists need to spend more time discussing the factors that bring affairs about in a relationship; and give time to discuss the emotional feelings and psychological states of the parties involved.

This affair took place over 20 years and 6 children ago. I still don't feel like my wife really came clean with me. I believe she carries around a lot of guilt because of it. Here is the twist . . . She sees a therapist for severe depression now. I fear she is having an affair with him. He has set me up to fail in this marriage, especially in our sex life. I feel helpless in this situation.

I, being a male, did not trust a female therapist.

I eventually found a female therapist who was helpful, I think the males thought I was exaggerating my depression.

Two therapists, a male and a female, should be available for support for both parties involved.

The most important aspect for me was to be able to find a therapist who I could trust after having my trust be broken. It was a wonderful thing to be able to talk to someone that was calm, could listen and be able to understand. But most of all, I looked at his relationship with his wife as he talked of her with great pride and love. I was able to realize that there are people that do respect and care for each other in a relationship.

Our male therapist tends to minimize the effects of an affair on a woman. It seems to be a "boys will be boys" attitude. They tend to pat you on the hand and say you will be just fine. Then you want to castrate both the therapist and your husband. You go for help and end up with yet another man who seems to think with both heads. I'm very tired of condescending men. My husband can continue seeing him, but I'm going to see a woman. NOT so I can hear what I want to hear, just to talk to someone who has the same frame of reference.

It would help me if a therapist would give some background history of his or her own personal life. I am not sure if an unmarried therapist or one who may indulge in their own dishonesties would necessarily be able to fully understand or relate to the full extent of the pain.

8. Don't expect the hurt party to forget the affair or "set it aside and go on."

Direct Quotes of Comments by Respondents:

Our first counselor was very impatient with me. He felt that because my husband had been honest in admitting that he had a long affair and had said he was sorry and said he loved me, I should be able to just move on. Even my husband felt that the counselor was too harsh. We found a new counselor who has helped us both see how devastating this whole experience has been and continues to be to both of us.

I believe that much more emphasis should be put on the healing process and the fact that the injured partner may forgive, but may never forget or be completely able to trust again.

Don't expect the offended party to just put it aside and begin the business of working out the mechanics of a "good marriage." Let the person who had the affair know that this is a long grieving process, and not to expect their partner to move on easily.

My therapist seems to INSIST that I put the affair behind me after only 5 months. What I'm going to do is put my THERAPIST behind me.

I was told to "let it go," that wanting to know the details was counterproductive and that I should focus on improving the marriage. Not saying that anything is wrong with those concepts, but I felt left hung out to dry and I, to this day, resent that.

My husband never hid his affair, just didn't acknowledge that it was an "affair." The counselors all thought that I should ignore it and get on with my life. Maybe intense sexual and physical involvement (including many "I love you's and sex) don't constitute an affair anymore?

My ex-husband started the first affair within 1 year of our marriage. We went to counseling, but the counselor did not want to talk very much about the affair and only kept telling me to get over it and move on. I could not forgive, it hurt too much. The counselor could not understand the pain and how deep it went. We saw the counselor for about a year. Finally I pushed it into the back of my mind and we continued to be married for the children's sake...but it was never the same. I regret at that point in my life that I did not divorce him and leave. It would have been better for everyone involved. Instead I stayed and we grew to slowly hate each other. After 14 more years, several more affairs and after my love had turned into all-out hatred, we finally split up. I went to a counselor to deal with the divorce and this time it was entirely different. This counselor not only understood why I had such pain, she was able to help me understand how to put it into perspective in my life. I was able to pretty much let go of the hurt and move on.

I feel no resolution from counseling. I'm told repeatedly to "get over it." I am frustrated and angry.

9. Help clients connect with others who have "been there."

Direct Quotes of Comments by Respondents:

I wish that I had known earlier-on WHAT was going to happen to me, such as: I would lose my sense of self-worth, I would lose my ability to trust, I would cry constantly, I would not be able to eat, I would be in agony, among other effects---and that these were COMMON to others in my situation. It is in finding that you are NOT alone in your actions, feelings and responses that you find the most strength. It is vital to let "patients" know all that. Most important though (and I cannot stress this enough) is finding others in your same situation. That is most crucial.

I believe it is very important to offer couples an opportunity to see a successful marriage. Even though my husband and I NEVER wavered on our commitment to our marriage. (Separation or divorce was not an option.) We desperately needed to see and talk to a success story. It made a huge difference in our ability to deal with the day-to-day struggles of restoration when we were able to do that. We are in the process of working with a marriage ministry in our area to form a support group for couples recovering from infidelity.

A support group was something that really helped me more than the therapist. All of the people there had similar problems, and just hearing how someone else handled them was a great help. Also knowing that you were not alone in your feelings and situations.

We have had a professional group experience, and of all the sources of help, this has been the most meaningful.

Anyone doing work with the subject MUST educate themselves on what support is available to people, i.e. support groups, names of books and authors, etc.

10. Be well-informed about affairs and provide good information.

Direct Quotes of Comments by Respondents:

I believe that therapists that deal with the subject have a responsibility to be well-versed in the issue of affairs. I feel strongly that neither of the therapists that my wife and I saw were up to speed in that area.

I've found that reading as much as I can find about affairs did help me to begin the healing process. Along with the talking and counseling that I do participate in, progress has been made in my recovery. I do believe that permanent scars will remain within me, despite the new growth and opportunities I have now and will work toward in the future.

I think that a counselor should help the couple realize WHY an affair took place in order to stop those feelings before they happen again. I know attractions happen…I don't like that they happen and I get very jealous, but that is something I need to work on.

He lacked current reading material and information on affairs. My personal research helped me more than the many visits to the therapists. On an individual basis, therapy was more positive since it focused on our individual viewpoints.

Counselors should discuss what caused the marriage to break down and what happened during the affair.

I would have found it helpful if either of our therapists would have given us some idea of what typical things couples go through after an affair has been discovered. We found out most of our info from reading various books. In hindsight, it didn't seem like either of our therapists were very educated in dealing with affairs. Is this typical?

Therapists should put more focus on responsibility/the fact that affairs do not just happen; it's a choice. And how difficult it is to regain trust.

11. Encourage honest communication and answering all questions.

Direct Quotes of Comments by Respondents:

I think that a counselor should encourage the person who had the affair to be honest and to finally tell the spouse about the entire scope of his/her extramarital activities. I know that my recovery has been hindered by my spouse's inability to acknowledge other affairs, in spite of my requests to tell me.

Therapists, please, please stress the importance to couples, that communication and honesty is VITAL to a marriage!!

Therapists need to constantly push for honesty. My wife is still in an emotional affair; I have no proof of a sexual one, but cannot rule that out yet. She is lying to me, our son, and to our counselor on an on-going basis. Have gone once to counseling since affair discovered.

During the years my wife was having an affair (before I knew about it), she went to counseling. We couldn't go together so that she could keep her secret. Life is better now only because I can relate to REALITY now. Unfortunately she still has the habit of years of holding herself distant enough to protect her secret.

I think that counselors need to focus more on talking about the affair in detail if the one who has been cheated on wants to know all of the details. They need to include the children in the healing process. They need to focus more on the needs of the one who had the affair to deal with their problems than to the one who didn't, but yet help the one who didn't have the affair without being objective about a lot of things and putting the blame on that person.
Therapists need to push (without really PUSHING) communication, no matter what. It is truly the BEST thing.

I think the person who had the affair should be encouraged to be honest. More painful than the affair is knowing there is someone and continually being lied to. It tends to chip away at you self-esteem, trust, and makes you suspicious of everyone. It's like everyone knows but you, even though that may not be the case. When you are married for a long time, the marriage becomes a separate living entity. The pain comes from somewhere deep inside, a place I didn't know existed in me. I'm not sure of my own values anymore. They don't seem to be important in these times. My husband had an affair almost two years ago. I felt it but he constantly told me I was suspicious for no reason. Finally it came out when he returned from a business trip and I found a condom in his suitcase. For 7 months he continued to deny. Finally I just withdrew and told him to find a lawyer and I would. He went to see a counselor. He continued to deny it. The counselor asked to see me, and I mentioned the infidelity to him, thus he assumed I was told by my husband, and he confirmed that my husband had told him this. Otherwise I don't know how long it would have taken my husband to tell me. I confronted him, and he finally admitted to it, with great pain. He said he made a terrible mistake and didn't want me to know, because he was so afraid that I would leave him. To his credit he has suffered, but I have suffered even more. It is still a very new hurt for me and I am doing my best to separate the affair from the person. He is not defined by the affair. He has been a good husband and father. I could have acted on my first instinct and filed for divorce. However, I would still have THIS pain plus the pain of divorce and I would still love him. So I decided to make a commitment with him to work this out. He doesn't understand that I have to get past this issue of the affair before I can feel whole again. In conjunction I am working on my marriage as it would be counterproductive to put it on hold. It's history to him, but not to me. I read "The Monogamy Myth" and it helped me to realize I wasn't crazy. In fact I'm probably a textbook case. I look forward to the day the pain will not come with almost every breath. I just wish people would know what the consequences will do to the person they are the closest to in this world, before they cross that line. Once crossed, it's done.

Nothing I have read or heard from the counselors has helped in dealing with his silence. We are unable to have any meaningful discussions because he just clams up and says nothing.

Our therapist was also fooled by my ex-husband in that he believed the affair was over when it was not. He did not support my ex being open with telephone records etc., until I began to have suspicions about the affair continuing. I feel like he did not encourage openness in the discovery process and felt any need for me to know this information was more a control issue on my part. This I think helped contribute to the ease of my ex continuing the affair.

Therapists must emphasize the honesty required for the spouse who had the affair. If the other spouse has a need for reasons of motivation behind the affair, this must be stressed and explored as the other spouse has a great need for understanding the whole aspect of the affair. By allowing the spouse who had the affair to bury his head in the sand saying that he 'just made a mistake' is a generality and not a tangible reason for any marriage to work towards mutual monogamy. As long as I hear this from my spouse, I will continue to feel as though he will continue to make mistakes as they are just that...'just mistakes' as he calls them. This is too vague and we cannot grow from this experience, even through a therapist's help.

You HAVE to talk it out to the victim spouse's satisfaction to have resolution to the affair. Anything less and there is no resolution.

Our first counselor focused on communications as being the cause of our problems. I did not see this as being constructive because I felt that I had tried to be communicative during the time that my husband was involved in the affair. I felt that the problem was his inability to talk to me and that he needed to seek help on his own to overcome his problem with communication and honesty. I think we could have been better helped by trying to discover how we differed in our views of marriage and monogamy and how those differences would have an impact on our marriage. My second counselor was much better in getting me on a track to rebuild my life and to live with the realization that my husband had had an affair. Whether or not he had needs that had not been met in our marriage was not the issue with my second counselor. The issue was to get me back on track with my life and to feel free to say what I think and to say what I need, regardless of what he feels or says.

Our counselor agreed with my husband that his past was a closed chapter. Then he eventually had us write letters to each other and changed the rules in the middle. So my husband says he'll talk, but then hides behind his alcoholism and says he doesn't remember. I need to resolve the past in terms of what was happening at times between us. The time frames he gives are too vague.

The counseling I/we received did not support my need to get all my questions answered. Because the counseling did not support this, my spouse feels totally justified in "putting it behind us and going forward; not living in the past." As far as I'm concerned this has made it very easy for him and extremely difficult for me.

Respondents' Responses re: more effective therapists

I would suggest to counselors to strongly suggest to the cheater that they must answer all the questions their spouse has. I would have been helped a lot more if my spouse did.

Counselors need to be emphatic with the person who had the affair that it is essential to tell the spouse about the affair, even if it's over, as well as all the details they want to know. The relationship, if it is to survive, must be built on complete disclosure to rebuild trust. That is the way our therapist (who was my husband's therapist initially) advised my husband, and I think it helped him to finally be honest with me.

A counselor should focus much energy on getting the betrayer to tell the whole truth.

I will never forgive our first therapist for saying to me "don't have an affair with the affair." She cut me off from my intuition and gave my husband a tool to conceal renewed extramarital activities. For two years I had suspicions that, when brought up, met the response "remember what the therapist said about...." My husband was terrified of what I would do if I found out. It was only after I developed debilitating insomnia and sought out a new counselor who focused on what I felt, not what I thought, that I got back in touch with my intuition. Our marriage began to crumble and my husband asked for a marriage counselor. Then the truth of the affairs over the last 6 years surfaced. Nine months later we are still with this therapist (we have "mine," "his," and "ours"), and he has been a tremendous value to us.

I'm seeing a psychotherapist now and she is taking me through step by step before I confront my husband on his current affair. This method has really helped me and I don't feel pushed into something when I'm not ready.

Therapists need to help the partner who had the affair own up to their responsibility in being honest, no matter what the pain or fear they maybe feeling. That they need to clearly understand the longer the secret goes on, the less likely the chance of the relationship surviving. The affair is something that needs to be talked through until both can feel comfortable again in the relationship if they are going to remain together.

Counseling didn't work as my ex lied. He kept me dangling until I woke up and decided I'd had enough so moved away from the area and divorced; best choice I ever made for my son and myself.

Help for Therapists

We were going to counseling before the affair for verbal abuse to the children, but it all was dealt with honestly and openly, truth is the beginning to healing.

In my situation, the counselors tended to focus on my spouse, he's a very powerful and believable person. He lied about ending the affair, and when the truth came out two years later the counselor apologized to me and said she believed he had ended it and realized how he had turned everything against me, saying it was all my fault. I would recommend time alone without the spouse to work through everything. I never had time alone with the counselor.

I found it very helpful when my counselor suggested I use a tape recorder to capture my ex-spouse's response to simple questions, to make me realize I was not the one in denial. I found phone bills, letters, condoms and such before finally meeting 3 of the women he had affairs with. The tape player helped when I was at my most vulnerable. We have been divorced for over a year now and he still denies the affairs.

I think therapists should stress more openness no matter what, especially discuss what may have caused it to happen and explain to the cheater why it's so difficult for the betrayed to let it go-- and also discuss that the cheater may have some real mental issues to figure out.

In my particular situation, I believe encouraging honesty regarding the affair would have helped me resolve my feelings much sooner. Because my spouse was told I probably would never get over the affair she is not willing to answer my questions. It has been 2 years, and while I love her more today than when we married, I don't know if I will ever completely get over what happened.

My husband has had six affairs that I know of in the 29 years of our marriage. The first five were buried and I endured. This time, however, we are both in individual therapy as well as couples counseling. Our current couples counselor is very good, but she insists that we are making a new beginning and should not dwell on the past. I feel that was the mistake we made in the early years of our marriage, because it has never been a dead issue for me. I would like to be unselfish and forgiving, but I'm feeling more and more a sense of self-preservation. I am fighting for honesty on both of our parts. I WANT a solid, loving intimate relationship with my husband.

Therapists need to concentrate first on getting the betrayer to face what he has done and how complete honesty about even the littlest details are needed for the betrayed spouse to heal.

Need to encourage honest communications at whatever cost to the relationship. I wasted precious years, money, and emotional fruitlessness on someone who did not respect me enough to be truthful.

There needs to be complete honest disclosure from the partner who had the affair. I am always wondering, "was he one of her affair partners," etc. - leaves a very bitter taste.

Therapist insisted adult children should be told nothing. Keep it behind closed doors. So much pain and hurt.... Married 30 years.

Once an affair is discovered I believe all nitty-gritty details should be confessed, feelings, activities, duration, etc.

The hardest part is facing the truth. Once told the truth, then there is an emotional eruption and then the relief begins to come. Nothing can make things better except honesty.

I think therapists might focus a little on whether or not the spouse is willing to admit that he had an affair, even when you have found proof. My husband liked to make me think that it was nothing and still to this day won't admit to more than a "secret" friendship. And since then I have discovered that he has had several more affairs. Women need to be a lot more aggressive with this, if they want to stay married, than I was.

Our counselor told my husband not to tell me ANY details of his affair because it would just hurt me more in the long run. However, I have had a hard time not knowing the details and continually questioning and wondering in my mind. I think I feel like he is still not being honest with me and that the counselor was saying it was ok.

12. Miscellaneous Comments about Therapists

Direct Quotes of Comments by Respondents:

I insisted that my husband and I see a counselor and I told him he could choose the one he felt most comfortable with. We saw two. Both were of his choosing but only because I insisted. Both times he decided not to go after about three visits. It was about the time he had to begin to talk about the affair and what made him have the affair. He only got angry and then would not go back. I really felt that in both cases, the counselors loved taking their fee ($90.00 and $125.00

each time) but really could care less whether we healed or not. I have yet to hear from either of them as to how we are doing.

The expense of counselors is out of this world. I think this is a major factor in many couples not getting the help they need during crisis times in their marriages.

Our counselor was more worried about finance than our well-being.

It would have been helpful if the therapists could have remembered more about what we had said or shared in each session.

The most difficulty I felt in counseling was that I felt judged and I felt judgment against my husband. My counselor constantly played the devil's advocate and did not give enough unconditional support. I was fortunate enough to have received it from a friend, and that is what I believe has gotten me through this. Unconditional support is the only thing that helped me feel o.k. about myself in this situation and gave me the grounding to figure out what I needed to do in my situation. Constantly pointing out the opposite or worst case scenario only confused me more than I already was.

Therapists, please do not take sides with either spouse. Ask honest and open questions no matter how painful the answers may be. Be very forward and straight to the point.

It would have helped me if he could have said he understood how I felt and that what I was feeling was normal or just something that was more supportive.

In my situation, my husband had an affair with a client (we have our own business). The client was a "friend" of mine and was involved in our personal life as well as business life. I felt like all aspects of my life were torn apart and I could go nowhere for refuge from the pain, i.e. work or home. Counselors need to be more knowledgeable about the practical aspects of self-employed individuals, and there seemed to be little help for me in continuing to run the business. I felt victimized and sad for a long time as my need to run my business (practical matters - and the need to have my husband not interact with the client) could not be met for a few months. It was hard.

My husband had an Internet affair that included actual meeting physically. I think more counselors need to learn about Internet affairs and the addiction element.

Therapy did not help, but a very dear friend is helping me and I now find I'm questioning myself as to whether I still am in love with him. Life is too short and I am just very unhappy. I may just need to move on regardless; I'm hoping for some answers to come to me.

We may not make it, despite very good counseling (still going on, but husband doesn't seem to be making any progress). I wish there were something that therapists could do for us in this situation. It is almost exclusively because of his hampered psychological development. His capacity level for full honesty, commitment, even love, is much lower than I ever imagined.

We went once every two weeks, and the sessions lasted 20 minutes each visit. I feel that was not enough counseling, and would have liked more time to talk. I would have liked to see my wife and I go to counseling once a week. Also, be more open to talk about a couple's sexual background together.

There were two affairs he had, one is still current for him. I've moved him out and am pending a divorce. I don't think counselors did enough for us. He is also too immature.

We just started marital counseling and it will be helpful to us. I am still angry at times and still in "shock."

In my case the counselor's help was limited not through her fault but because (as I expected) my husband wasn't able to go beyond the 5th session. A person that usually has difficulty talking about his problems or feelings to others, going for counseling and actually continuing for 5 sessions was something even I wasn't expecting. However, at the same time, still very much involved with the other woman (and trying to hold onto anything he could find or imagine about me that could have lead to his affair, and not feeling guilty for it), he started feeling that even the counselor was against him. (He realizes now that he was the one against himself). Since we went to only 5 sessions, the counselor didn't really enter into the affair - (it was supposed to come later) - because at that time he was using the "I want to leave this marriage because I don't love you anymore…the affair has nothing to do with what I feel." Do she was addressing that "I don't love you anymore" issue first. For me though, the only help I felt I got was in diffusing potential "flammable" discussions. One of the reasons why I suggested counseling was because we would start talking about our situation, he would start stating all the things that he felt had lead to it, I would try to rationalize the whole thing, try to show him he was overreacting to things that should have been addressed before, but weren't so serious that would completely destroy any feeling he might have had for me, he would start feeling defensive and we would get stuck. In counseling we were able to address those issues with the counselor redirecting when needed. In terms of coping strategies, or ways to deal with the problem itself, basically all that she suggested I had already tried or was in the process of trying, so it didn't give me any new tools to deal with the situation.

Our therapist was great, but never convinced my husband to admit he needed help, and to continue counseling. I wish the therapist would have persisted with "counseling cannot end, until we all discover WHY!"

I think affairs are the most destructive thing that can happen in a marriage. It completely erodes the base on which it was built. After the first time, I never trusted my first husband. I was suspicious all the time. And he always left clues so that I would find out. He took stupid chances over and over again. But I didn't have the ego-strength to leave him. And strangely, I still loved him. I had no idea how I'd support myself if I left. Now I could do so easily. I finally realized in therapy that what I experienced all those years was emotional abuse. But I sure wouldn't have called it that at the time.

I think there should be some sort of law, that forces couples to go to so many weeks of counseling before a divorce is allowed.

My therapist encouraged me to watch sad movies which really gave me an outlet for sadness, that I was unable to access through my anger. That was her most helpful contribution.

The therapist was to the point and skillful, but was treading on some of my husband's personal issues that had nothing to do with me; this was agitating my husband as I think he had never really been forced to examine his own behavior under a professional therapeutic "light."

When the therapist talked of maturity and responsibility, of giving "feelings" too much weight...he walked out of therapy, saying he didn't want to be mature. Period. That was the last of our therapy together. He only wanted to be there to convince me to approve of his choice for divorce. He ran away from his discomfort. Sad.

I believe his willingness to work with us without structured, or easy but short-sighted rules of behavior has precipitated a lot of soul-searching. My husband has actually had two affairs since we started counseling together, and our therapist has helped us to grapple with the "why's" and steered us clear of the destructive patterns in which we had previously engaged. The "I promise not to have any affairs while in counseling" approach would have felt much safer for me, but we would never be learning to free ourselves from our current operating modes. Trust is still a huge issue, but I feel a closer bond with my husband than ever before.

For people with religious faith, therapists need to encourage them to explore their feelings and the commitments they made. Revisit the foundation that their life is built on.

My husband had an affair with a good friend. I think a therapist should look into the dynamics of a "triangle" deal. How a spouse accepts friends into their family, the trust and the betrayal that is involved.

About a month ago, I found out about my husband's third affair. I am seeing a counselor, but he isn't yet. I am in the process of building my self-esteem to make a decision about this marriage. I am more likely not to remain married if I don't get more than words and no action. He has to work at this because I am getting stronger each day in my resolve to improve my chances of developing healthy relationships in the future.

The therapist says to make the healing about the two of us; that the other woman is out of the picture; but that is very difficult. The time and affection taken away from me is more hurtful than the physical betrayal. I want my husband to see her as the controlling, mean, hurtful, manipulative person she is, but he doesn't. I worry that she will always hold a piece of his heart. I have wonderful days and then can have a day filled with sadness, anxiety and tears. We will make it.

Presently we are back living together (we were separated for four months) because we have a newborn son that he is helping me care for along with our 3 year old son. I would like to try marriage counseling again but it is not clear whether he will be staying or leaving again.

I got him to a counselor through his company 3 times, and then he refused to go back. (He had all the answers, he didn't need counseling.) Right! The counselor said that my husband was in denial and an alcoholic (which he is), and that he wouldn't talk to "me" anymore until "I" went to Alanon.

I feel culpability for the failure. My husband said that it was my fault (My therapist said it wasn't). My self image has suffered a lot. I am afraid of the future.

Help for Therapists

I had a great therapist. She recommended my husband seeing another therapist. Too bad he didn't take the advice earlier. Maybe we could have been saved. What I know today I should have forced him into seeing another therapist (he sees now). The scars are too severe.

We both went for counseling, but my husband felt that it was very intrusive, he's a very private person, and that it wasn't at all helpful. Since he was dealing with a different situation than me, namely one of great loss, I would have hoped that a counselor could have been of greater help with this aspect.

Other Topics included in the Comments from Respondents

Despite the fact that all the "comments" were to focus on suggesting ways that therapists could be more effective in their work with affairs, many of the comments addressed other important topics, providing additional insights into effectively dealing with this issue. So these Other Topics were organized into 18 categories and reproduce the direct quotes from the respondents under each topic below.

Preparation for Marriage

Suspecting/Confronting

Denial

Discovering

Devastation

Why

Third Party

Deciding

Separating

Divorce

Staying Married

Children

Anger

Talking

Honesty/Lying

Trust

Forgiving

Personally Recovering

Preparation for Marriage

Get the word out about prevention. Focus on marriage and relationship education. Talk about affairs - don't keep it hidden. Help destroy some of the myths about affairs. Help premarital couples affair-proof their marriage. Test couples to predict the likelihood of an affair.

We met and married in a church. There wasn't any real pre-marital counseling. Looking back now, I should have been more assertive about dealing with the problems, instead of waiting for things to change.

There should be more premarital counseling and it wouldn't hurt if there was a waiting period after you decide you want to get married.

I believe it is only by talking openly in the family about dynamics, being honest, can the chain be broken in the generations.

Suspecting/Confronting

When I initially suspected my husband of having an affair and I confronted him with my suspicions, at first he denied it but then he said he had a one-night stand. So, I was dealing with that and trying to cope and rebuild but he was very angry, belligerent and I couldn't understand it. Come to find out, in the two months between when he admitted his "one night stand" (which never actually occurred) and my discovery of his affair, he was continuing his relationship with this other woman and pushing me for a separation. Now he is sorry and wants to make our marriage better.

My relationship was difficult due to the nature of my spouse's job where he often traveled, and I just had blind faith that he was doing what he needed to do for his family. I also worked and raised our three children. It was his 2-3 week absences that made me suspicious, and when I questioned him, he said nothing. I can talk and communicate to a mouse, but with my husband, it was most difficult. I believe he feels much guilt, but he will not talk.

I'm suspicious that another affair may be occurring.

When I left my husband, I knew nothing about the affairs. It was not until our final court date that I found out.

I was so surprised by my husband's non-sexual affair (had no clue), but I will never be that "surprised" again.

I actually confronted my wife with the affair when she was at a conference with the other lover. Recovery was immediate for me when she simply acknowledged the affair. The sense of relief allowed me to concentrate on her well-being. When she returned we were able to be completely open about it. In fact I encouraged her to call "the other" and help him through the separation. Incredibly, the affair has actually been a positive experience for both her and me.

It has been 6 months since confronting my husband, still don't know if my marriage will work. On his part, guilt etc…not a happy place.

A friend encouraged my husband to tell me. He didn't tell me on my own.

Denial

My husband continuously denied having affairs, he never admitted to it even after the divorce.

My spouse has continued to deny the affair, even though I contracted an STD from him.

My husband is in complete denial and never talks about it and if the subject comes up, he is either angry or acting like that period of time in his life never happened.

I was told on three occasions (about six months apart each) that the affair was over, but it continued for two years. Still not sure if it's really over.

I am particularly bothered by the way he went about this. The sneaky, deceiving ways that he chose to use. The secret money, the secret Internet mailboxes, etc. Truly, he shouldn't have been caught. There wasn't any way for me to prove my suspicions. After three months of going round and round about this, I finally found some printed Email under the floormats in his truck. I should never have found this. It was a complete "fluke!" I was intending to detail the interior of his truck, as an added Father's day present. This was to go along with the floor mats that I had already bought for his truck. Huge error! But truly, he had covered his bases "unbelievably well."

My problem with this is: He could decide to do this again, and I'd really have no way of finding out due to the level of his concealing practices. Before I found the evidence, this time, he was comfortable in telling me that I was "delusional," rather than coming clean with any or all of his activities. This is the part that I find to be particularly unforgivable! I think it was more cruel than what he actually was doing. Also, because he was so very good at concealing everything, and the "fluke" that led me to the truth (this time), I can't be sure that this was the first time he's done this. I am inclined to believe that he's been untrue all along, but I think that is just because I'm feeling like such a fool now. But truly, the way that he's covered his bases, it is entirely possible and not entirely improbable. At this time I feel unable to trust him. I feel that if I did trust him again, I'd be a bigger fool than before, and I'd deserve whatever came along next. I don't think that I'd ever be able to trust him. This is due to the "expert" way that he chose to go about all of this, and the unlikely way that I did eventually find the truth to this one episode of his life. I am truly torn at this point. One detail that I can't overlook is our 9 year old son. Leaving him is not an option for me. I don't think it would be for him (his father) either. His father is very involved in his life! He even coaches him in Little League (for the last five years) and also participates in Boy Scouts with him for the last three years. I would hate to split them up, but like I said, "leaving my son behind is not an option." Every time I look at my husband, I just think about how "OK" he was with having me believe that I was delusional. I'm wondering if this wasn't the beginning of having me committed to some institution after fully convincing me that I was delusional. I am the type that would want to have this condition treated and have myself fully recovered at any length of time required. I wouldn't want to be going through my life without a grip on "reality." I would be inclined to go along willingly. This scares the heck out of me. I believe that his methods of concealing any information were far, far above the norm. I believe that he was also extremely cruel to me by suggesting that I was delusional. I also believe that his conscience wasn't suffering in the least during the entire time that this was going on. I came to wonder if maybe I weren't delusional. I am rambling on now, and I could continue to ramble on. I'm not going to. I will cut this off now. I am terribly troubled at this crossroads in my life, and still have yet to choose a direction to take.

My wife is a sex addict, as her family and father as well. This only complicated everything for me. She followed as a true SA, though with not wanting a divorce to destroy the family BUT to use divorce as a tool of intimidation to make me coward to her. Didn't work. During this time, I applied myself to digging in to the past to learn what it was. This is where I found calm and forgiveness. It wasn't easy by any means, but it did give me a totally different understanding on life. Because the SA thing seems to be so prevalent in our/her family, I am petrified with what will happen to my children later in life. This has driven me to end this once and for all, whichever way it goes, marriage or divorce. I really couldn't ever feel good knowing what I know about this and let it go without doing something about it. If there is a divorce, I know I'll have a war on my hands to surface all the secrets that plague our family now for three generations. But it is these secrets along with the deceit and lies that have forced everyone into denial and not to be able to see it as it is.

He denies it still, even after I confronted her and she admitted everything. He says it was on-line, no actual contact, but disappeared for a few days and will not give any explanation on where he was or with whom; just says he never has cheated and he wasn't with her.

Discovering

This is real new, only two weeks that I know about it. I found out only because the lover was upset about their breakup. He came to my house and my spouse was forced to tell me.

On New Year's Eve my husband got me drunk and then he told me. I was shocked.

While looking through phone bills (that never previously came to the home), I found out about various women. I am up to 11 now. All kinds. Shapes. Colors. I have been heartbroken ever since.

My husband's affair was with my best friend during the first three years of our marriage. He did not tell me until the tenth year of our marriage, fully seven years after the affair had ended. He only told me because he wrongly suspected and accused me of having an affair with a male friend who was going through a divorce. He now feels relieved for telling me.

I found out about my ex-wife's affair after we were divorced. I realized she was having an affair after she moved into an apartment and her upstairs neighbor was her boss. Her reasoning for the divorce was that she didn't love me anymore and that when I came home from business trips, she told me that I was "disrupting" the household. I never thought it was an affair.

I found out about the affair 4 years later...but at the time of the affair I had strong suspicions and asked many times if he was. He always lied to me and said I was insane...I felt 'insane' not knowing for sure. At that time...I got a phone call from someone 4 years after it ended...so I feel that if I found out while it was actually happening...I wouldn't have felt lied to and maybe I could have dealt with it more effectively. I really was in shock when I got the call...mostly because I felt lied to for years and that my husband could really lie to me. I felt as if I never really knew him. So, to me, if someone wants an answer...it is helpful to tell the truth. My husband was carrying this guilt around for 4 years and our marriage was strained from it. We are now much better because there are no lies between us...although I did want to know more details but he refused to tell me. So I would say that details must be answered if a person really wants to know them. He had an intense anger at my questions...which was hard because I never discussed this with anyone...not family or friends. We went to a counselor right away...but was turned off by the lack of concern...so, we never returned to counseling. After 2 years the pain has subsided...but I still feel sick when I pass the place that I believe it happened. Also, when I am making love with my husband...sometimes I picture him and her...and I feel sick...but things are definitely better.

When I learned about the affairs, they had been over for 10+ years. One affair lasted 2 years, the other only months. Both fizzled on their own. He is trying.

I discovered my wife's affairs 25 years after they were over. She was in the middle of the first affair AT THE TIME WE WERE MARRIED. She went straight to the second when the first ended. It was for "solace" - after all, she couldn't talk with ME about it. Each affair lasted about 2 years. Life was hellishly confused then. She seemed to get "better" after it was over.

I am just 2 and 1/2 months from finding out. We still have many unresolved questions and issues.

It happened only 3 months ago that I found out, but the affair was over 3 years ago.

For 7 years I tried to be patient and show love, hoping that he would change. Our marriage has had its ups and downs (separations) but I finally felt we had conquered it. Then last week I was notified by another husband that his wife had been seeing my husband. How do I go through this again?

My ex-husband's affairs were all with men. After twelve years of marriage, I finally discovered he was gay. There needs to be more help out there for this astonishingly large group of "straight spouses." At this time, the resources are very limited.

My spouse continues to have online relationships, there have been at least 50 woman since the affair that he talks to on AOL, and has what I guess they call cyber sex.

My spouse went through a period of alcohol abuse and got involved with his secretary because he felt sorry for her. It was also good for his ego, which must constantly be "fed." He was involved with her for 3 years, broke up with her and stopped drinking. About 18 years later I confronted him with what I thought had probably been a one night stand and was shocked to learn that he had been so deeply involved. I would have left him if the affair had been for any other reason than pity and ego. The woman he was involved with turned out to be seriously mentally ill, is still with her husband and is on disability, but while she was involved with my husband she kept him in the affair with tantrums and rages. The only way I ever finally admitted to myself that there had been an affair was her obscene phone calls, and it took me a long time to recognize her voice.

Devastation

After three years of the discovery, I still suffer from devastation feelings from time to time; and feel I haven't being able to get over it. But on the other hand, I feel I love him.

It is still very painful to even think about how I was betrayed, let alone discuss it at length. I am, however, trying to deal with it one day at a time.

There is no greater pain than betrayal by one you considered your best friend....

I realize that the affair would never have happened if our marriage had been on track in the first place, but that thought doesn't always take away the pain.

The pain and loss take away that innocent pure feeling in life.....it is like a death. I still find in all that I have read too many excuses for the one who betrayed. It almost seems too easy for them...while the pain is so deep and rich, it never really goes away.

My husband told me of two one-night flings...just before I had surgery for breast cancer...out of the blue. Some discussion…renewed vows...things got better for awhile. He pretty much thinks I am over it I guess. He knows I am depressed but I really don't think he puts it together with what he told me. He says one time was early in our marriage and he was drunk. He says the other was 13 or 14 years ago when we were in a business with lots of financial problems and stress. I think he hasn't told me all of what he has done. I know he has had very close friendships with various women through the years and always told me that he had never cheated and never would, but obviously he lied. I don't know why he chose to tell me at that time, but I couldn't really deal with it because of the surgery and radiation so I just went along with the "I'm sorry" stuff and now I am having to deal with all of the real feelings. Even though it supposedly happened years ago, and before we became Christians, it might just as well have been yesterday in my heart. I have something dead in me now and sometimes I really don't even care about him or anything. I have not seen a counselor yet, but am going to see one soon through an employee assistance program from work, because I am on medication and I still have horrible depression and I cry a lot when I am alone, which is most of the time as he is self employed and works seven nights a week. I also am much more aware of the fact that women are attracted to him.

My husband had a long-term (over 10 years) phone-sex/explicit letters type of affair with a former sex partner of my husband's. They previously had a physical relationship (prior to our marriage) and then stayed in contact for almost our entire marriage of 11 years. He has no emotional feelings for her; in fact, he thinks she is a total slut. She used to "service him orally" and they only had intercourse 2 times as he said he didn't trust her or care for her in any way; or so he says. It is almost like having a long relationship with a prostitute or 1-900 worker except he did know her and had previously had a physical sexual relationship with her. Nonetheless, it is totally devastating to me to know that he deceived and betrayed me for such a long period of time.

I discovered the affair about ten months ago. I had some difficult periods, particularly about four to five months after discovery. During that period I was very depressed. I blamed myself a lot. My spouse seemed to avoid any responsibility for the affair. This made me feel as though I must have been a major cause for her entering the affair. I felt inadequate and now a "second choice" since she apparently had traded me for another and only after I found out about the affair did she leave him.

I had been married for 23 years when I was told by my spouse about his affairs (11 of them). I had the greatest marriage in the world. I was extremely happy and often counted my lucky stars. I never suspected. He has no excuse for his behavior. He said that was how he thought he was supposed to act. Be a good spouse, father, etc., and have affairs on the side. I feel that I will never get over this. It has been two years. I love my husband. He is a wonderful person. He says that he will never have another affair...he would rather die first than to hurt me again. I wish I could close my eyes and all of this would just disappear. But I know that will never happen. Somehow, I will learn to live with this broken heart.

Other Comments from Respondents about Therapists

Any extramarital affair is the worst thing that one spouse can do to another. It has been over seven months and I don't think I will ever get over it.

The most violating, destructive event in my life. So many lives were changed due to this one event.

I will never know... what is the truth... This is worse than dying.

I guess I should qualify my remarks by saying that all of my husband's affairs were with other men. He felt that he was bisexual. The affairs went on for nine years out of a twelve-year marriage. I was just as devastated to lose my marriage to other men as to another woman. It was the loss of a dream of a great family life.

This has been the most hurtful time I've ever experienced. It completely devastated me for 2 years.

A month before we got married, he tried many times to sleep with a friend of mine. Even on my wedding day, he told her he had to behave that day because he was getting married but he told her that he didn't have to in the future. They never had sex but he pursued having sex with her and she refused. For me, this is cheating even if they haven't had sex. What I have a hard time dealing with is the "betrayal." I never thought he could go behind my back. What makes it even worse is that he ruined the nice memories of our wedding day.

The affair involving my wife was an on-line affair. While all indications clearly show there was never any actual contact, the pain is just as great as if there were. It was with someone known to both of us, and who I considered a friend (certainly not any more!). She stopped immediately when I confronted her, but I still shudder every time she goes on the computer, even though I know nothing is going on.

I sometimes feel I'm the only one who can't let go of my husband's affair. I know other people have experienced affairs, but my anger and resentment will not go away. It is the most devastating thing I've ever faced in my life, I want to get over this now and I'm afraid I never will. I believe it takes time, but I feel trapped in my own feelings. It has affected my everyday life in so many ways; I've become a moody person, and I never used to be.

It has been within the past 2 months that I have found out. The hurt was so tremendous that I couldn't deal with anything for a while. Only in the past couple of days have I realized it wasn't just done to me, it was done to us. So now that the self-pity has subsided I hope I will begin to really focus on the whole picture. My brain as you can tell still has a long way to go before it thinks normally again.

I grieved just like after losing a loved one to death. The pain would wash over me again and again in waves when least expected. What dies is an essential innocence and trust deep inside. The knowledge is more painful than anyone can imagine, because it is also linked to still loving that person. I wanted to punish him, but could not bring myself to hurt him. I felt a great deal of guilt too. Putting things back together is not so easy as one thinks. It worked for a long time, but I felt like I was the only one trying. He seemed to want to forget it ever happened and not deal with the ramifications on life for more than a short period of time.

This was THE most painful experience of my life. I, too, had affairs in the past and had I known at that time that this would come back to me later in life, I would NEVER, EVER have done it.

It still just plain hurts that the two people I was closest to could just cut me out.

Most of my continuing pain comes from being unable to reconcile the kind and good person that I have and do believe my spouse to be with the person that could have so misled me and the other woman whom he planned to marry after somehow extricating himself from our marriage. I have the terrible sense that nothing is really secure or permanent.

I was in such an emotional wreck, that it is by the grace of God, and with the help of my family, that I survived.

Even though it has been almost 2 years since I discovered the affair, I still cannot put it behind me where it does belong, and where my husband wants it. He can't seem to understand why I can't just let it go. I will never be the same person again and the past 2 years have been a real hell for me, since I never really thought this could happen and I was absolutely in shock and numb and filled with rage because of the extent of the lies and deceit and just devastated.

I was totally devastated when I found out about both of my husband's affairs going on at the same time or one right after the other over a one-year period.

I cannot really put into words the pain and agony this type of situation can put on someone. I know for me it is a daily struggle. The humiliation of this experience and my partner telling me he wasn't sure how much he loved me until he made the dreaded mistake was more than I could bear.

My husband's affair was 1 month online and 1 actual meeting without a sexual encounter. Still I felt all the same emotions and devastation that many people do with long-term or continuous affairs.

My husband's affair started as an online "flirting friendship" and they secretly met and their relationship became sexual. The other woman lived in a different state, so it involved a lot of money and a lot of lying and secrecy. I was also 7 months pregnant with my second child at the time!

It's been a year but I still seem consumed by thoughts of what happened. My husband seems to be trying to make things right, but I still feel so sad. We are getting along better than we ever did, but I still have a lot of pain that I can't seem to let go of.

I feel that people expect me to have moved on further than I have. I think that you need ongoing support for a long time after the affair.

I asked my husband to call her from our speaker phone to tell her that he does not love her, that this was all wrong, and that he doesn't want to lose me or his children; that we are all that matter to him in his life, but he will not do it. I am hurting terribly, can't sleep, can't eat, and basically I'm dying from inside out.

Why

Affairs are a complex occurrence.... and I believe don't usually happen for any one reason. It is wise to look at many things when trying to analyze what to do and how to deal with all the repercussions affairs produce.

In certain situations as in mine knowing an actual why it happened more than once (with the same person) would be helpful because he says he doesn't know!

It's hard to know that after 36 years of marriage I was replaced for a time by a younger woman and I don't know why. He says he doesn't know why either.

16 years later, and multiple other affairs, I'm still struggling to understand why! I love him, he loves me, life is good, so I stay.

My husband had an affair with a coworker. I'd always trusted him; in fact that was a reason I married him. He's said there were multiple reasons for the affair: pressured into it at work due to teasing, time away from me, he always thought I'd have an affair, lack of self-esteem, etc.

The affair lasted 2 weeks. He saw her 2 times, but they started out as a friendship, so I am still new to all this. We are working on our marriage, we have 3 children, I still love him and I believe he loves me. I think he was curious what it felt like; I don't know, he said it was only sex he wanted.

To this day I am trying to get my wife to tell me the reason for her affair. My neighbor, who was supposed to be my wife's friend, told me that her husband and my wife were having an affair. I had an idea something was going on. She wrote him numerous love letters on the computer and in her ignorance left them on there for the world to see. I really think that she loves me but she can't help being the way she is.

Sorting through this type of betrayal has been tough, because you are dealing with a person who has done an about-face on his perception of life compared to what he had been like before. I am dealing with a man who says he has always been a rebel, and now he is on this path again. He claims that Life and Society took him off this path 30 years ago, when he settled down, married me, had a family (4 kids) and worked in developing a highly successful business. Oh well. He is in therapy with the other woman, so they "won't make the same mistakes." Ironic, when I wonder if the therapist ever asked them if they were married to other people at the time. (They were).

I searched for reasons why the affair occurred. My husband went through the illness and death of his father and became very distant towards me. The mistress was an old girlfriend who made herself available to the point of an obsession over him. Had it not been for my faith, I don't think I would have been able to forgive him. My spouse was my very best friend; he shut me out for about six months to the point of total rejection.

Other Comments from Respondents about Therapists

I became lost in my work and failed my wife. I do not take responsibility for her affairs, but I do take responsibility for my part in getting to the place where that could happen.

My husband was unhappy with himself...not the marriage so much, but himself. He came to realize this later, but at the time blamed me...I was an easy scapegoat. One area where I do take responsibility is that I let my role of equality in the relationship slip. I stayed home to have children and somehow bought into the belief that he as the primary breadwinner was somehow more important than I. I became the keeper of the house and children...we stopped doing that together...I failed in making myself see that I was of equal importance as he was in the relationship.

I can't speak for everyone else, but I think that communication (open communication) is vital in a relationship. No matter what the fear... "my wife would divorce me if she found out...", "my husband wouldn't understand my attraction for another man," or whatever the reason for secrets may be, I truly believe that is what kept myself and my husband from truly making our marriage work. I seem to feel that it was all my fault... not skinny enough after having the kids, not into sex as much as before the kids, not asking enough about his work, not having a spotless house all of the time... the list goes on and on. My husband reassures me (or at least tries to tell me) that none of this was my fault. I know that he was scared to talk to me at the point in our relationship when the affair took place. He says he was angry at me because I didn't "appreciate" his efforts as a provider and husband. That is a two-way street, however. He started the relationship with this woman at work about a year before sex entered the picture. When I was 3 months pregnant with our second child, he bought this other woman a necklace "just to put a smile on her face." What about a smile for his wife? I think the attraction started very early on for my husband. He still "doesn't know" why he bought the necklace or his feeling behind any of the actions. He claims the sex wasn't as fulfilling as ours, she wasn't physically wonderful, and they didn't have "wild sex," just "normal" sex. I wonder why he went back time and time again. If he was having the guilt every time AFTER the act of sex, why go back? He still can't answer that question. He says he felt sorry for her at the beginning because she was going through a tough divorce from an abusive husband. Maybe he was her Knight in Shining Armour. Who know? Maybe I will never know the true feelings behind this relationship. I think that he has a lot of discovery to do within himself before he can be truly open with me again.

My husband himself says he got "lost;" he hit his mid-thirties and said "is this it?" ...he wanted some excitement some variety. He got it for awhile but he traded that for his loss of personal self-respect and integrity. He would be the first to tell you now that it was not worth it...people/friends will never see him the same way, nor will I. I love him but not the way I did...perhaps I idolized him too much and now I know he is human and can make poor choices and choices that are totally self-centered.

After 22 years of marriage, I never dreamed my husband would have an affair. We had a wonderful sexual relationship and seemed to get along fine. A contributing factor may be the onset of his sexual dysfunction, which he came to me about a few months before he started his affair. He sought medical help but it didn't really help. Would not even think of trying Viagra because of fear for his health. It wasn't long after that he started up an affair with his ex-wife and then someone else, both being in his age group. I am 13 years his junior.

People cheat more when they think their mate has to meet every one of their needs, or another person should, rather than try to find a way to meet their own needs.

After his last affair, 3 years ago, is when I realized I was not in love with him any longer, and am having my own first affair. Its funny now I feel like he would never cheat on me again, and feel I can actually trust him for the first time, but it's still to late.

My husband and I seem to have a different focus, and different communication styles, which make it near impossible to resolve this issue...he wants to move on, and I want to understand how it happened.

I believe most affairs begin because of something emotional that is not being met either by the person themselves or in the relationship with their spouse. We are all individuals with our own personal needs, and if someone is unable to express when their personal emotional needs are not being met, I believe we tend to look for some way to compensate for this need and in some cases another person SEEMS to fill this need. But when we choose this route of compensation, we only create more emotional problems to deal with, and the one the whole affair started over also still exists and is usually passed on to the new relationship. We must learn first to express our wants and desires to our significant other before they can possibly even attempt to fill them...most of us cannot read the minds of our spouses. We know, most times, when there is something bothering them, but unless they are willing and the other person interested enough to HEAR and listen to what they have on their mind, there is no way this need can be met or any other resolution can be found to fix the problem. We all must learn that an affair doesn't fix anything for anyone, it only creates a bigger problem, even when we think expressing our honest feelings may hurt our loved ones, we must still do it, because the result of festering an emotional wound can be so much more devastating.

My spouse had an affair with a much younger man that she had met at her workplace. Of course, I blame her for the affair, but blame both of us for the deterioration of the marriage. I feel that I did not love her the way I should have and feel that she did not communicate with me.

Third Party

The affair surfaced 5 weeks ago. Their friendship developed 4-5 weeks prior. She still feels that she has the right to speak and (possibly) see him to talk since they are friends. He is married with 2 young kids. Told her today that I can't keep hope in saving our marriage if she still wants to have contact with him. She didn't like that at all. Became cold. Told her that if she wants the marriage to end, then by continuing contact is the way to do it. Told her that he can't help us work on our marriage...we have to do that ourselves.

Part of the pain of the situation was intensified by the harassment and games the woman started (harassing phone calls, email, veiled threats). She did not want my husband, she just wanted to cause pain and try to collect money. She continued her harassment for months until we had enough evidence of it to have our lawyer state that any further contact would result in legal action against her. No word since. Most events during the affair were geared towards gathering damaging information.

Most of my anger is toward the other person (not my spouse). They need to suffer for the pain they caused to me. I don't know if I will ever be able to get over it.

It has been difficult because the other man lives in our neighborhood, attends the same church and has children in the same school as us. We continue to be reminded of the affair because we still see him regularly.

Of course, everyone is going to wonder what the sex was like with the other person and that is very difficult to overcome. I got very turned off during sex one night because I got the image of my husband looking down at this other woman the way he was looking at me. "Was it the same," "How did he feel emotionally when he was with her"...I can't shake those feelings. He still works with this person and she lives in the same town. I'm starting to feel like I want revenge on this person which shocks me because I really haven't felt ill will towards her even during my husband's detailed descriptions of the affair. This confused my husband. He thought that I would want to go out and run her down with my car. I don't. I met with her and talked to her. She provided me with information my husband would have never told me. I told him that we should really thank her for causing this trouble in our life if it makes for a stronger, more loving marriage. He disagrees. He would like to be the one to run her over. This also confuses me because I feel like that might just be hidden feelings for her that he just doesn't want to confront right now.

After I learned of the affair, I contacted his "lover" and she sent me a box full of cards and gifts he had sent her. He travels frequently and met her only on "business" trips. He still travels and I fear he's meeting someone every place he goes. I think I learned too much about his affair through the affiliation with his lover, hence the painful daily reminders since I know she's been to Arizona, been in my house, car, touched my dog.... My husband has always been in need of affirmation of his attractiveness to women. It started a year after we were married. I ignored the situation feeling secure since we were married but soon lapsed into depression and began building a wall around myself. This chased him away eventually, so I forgive him for searching for "her," but I'm still angry and resentful that he actually gave himself the approval to lie to me.

Please be careful of fulfilling fantasies. One spouse, in my case my wife, may decide they like being with other men (black) and as the saying goes "once they go black they never go back" is definitely true. Signed, wimp white husband whose white wife has a black lover.

Affairs are built on secrecy and dishonesty...they take place in an environment where 'real life' is not part of the mix...no one has to wash the floors pay the bills, clean a dirty diaper or any of the day-to-day monotony of living. The involved parties look their best, present only a facade of who they are...oh to be seen as a perfect partner...almost anyone can do this in the context of an affair but add real life to the mix and the picture isn't quite so perfect anymore.

Deciding

After more than two years I am very confused and unsure of whether to divorce or stay.

My husband cheated, and after 3 months decided he couldn't live with the guilt. He told me everything, and said he wanted to come back. I said I would be willing to work on things but since then he has gone back and forth on whether or not he really wants to stay married. We are both going to counseling but there is no change; he is still trying to decide whether or not to stay married.

I think at first that everyone wants to fix the relationship no matter what. I think it would be helpful to make people realize that what they want back is the relationship that was there before all of the lies and cheating. Things will never be the same. You either have to decide if it is something that you can live with and try to work things out or that it is something you could never live with. I personally feel that the person my husband is now is not the man I want to spend the rest of my life with. At first I wanted him back no matter what, but I didn't want the person he had become. I wanted the person and the relationship we had before and that can never be, so I had to mourn my loss and try to get on with my life.

I still feel like I'm stuck in neutral with the engine running! I've been hurt, but I can't hurt back. It's my nature or the way I grew up, I guess. I want a divorce, but that would hurt the feelings of so many people in the family, so I just exist day by day. I have no plans for the future, I hate to look back at the past and I really don't care if I wake up the next morning. I have enough money to survive, but no desire to get a job, or improve my situation.

My husband is still in phone contact with the other woman and has seen her once last fall. I consider the affair to be ongoing since they still talk. Although they are not in physical contact (she lives in Chicago we are in NYC), I still believe that it is possible unless he gives it up and recommits, which he has not done. (She recently expressed an interest to come and visit). My husband is still very much confused. Last Thursday he came home adamant that it was over and he would not start it again, but the thoughts of ending it over the weekend were too much and I don't believe he has done it. I also believe that depression plays a major role in this whole cycle of affairs. My husband clearly seeks her and other women in the past as a diversion to how crummy he feels much of the time. He does take anti-depressants. But every little thing is a major obstacle and has become more so in middle life. He does have individual therapy. My husband has gone through his whole life with a negative thinking pattern. Although I see it now, I didn't recognize how much this casts a shadow over his whole life. He doesn't remember good times easily but sure remembers the negative. He is rarely content with himself or his life and therefore our marriage, etc. We do not fight and I have always been supportive. Looking at this objectively, we have a good life and marriage by most people's standards. However, since he is never content he is not with this either. He always needs a new toy or believes the grass is greener some place else. Since I don't believe in divorce and can see things from a more optimistic point of view, I have held on longer than many would. He has known the present other woman for 4+ years. I do have to be honest and question will it ever get better at this point? This is what I must decide. Until the affair we didn't talk about these issues but we have good communication about it all now. Although I have not put my foot down and said "enough," he knows how I feel about it and that I am reaching the end of my patience. I am not in denial about the situation. I feel the circumstances and the fact that he is in therapy gives me hope that we can go on. I still believe that my husband and I can survive this, create a new relationship and find mutual happiness. He still believes something is missing, but I say it is him. Him being present, a participant and learning to be content with himself and the wonderful life he has. Depression, though, often keeps him from seeing this.

All I can say is not many marriages can last through affairs. If I had to do mine over today, I would get a divorce and move on. Life is too short to go through all the heartaches you go through. You lose the trust you once had and you don't know if you'll ever get it back. You always wonder if it could happen again.

People need to be cautious of the advice they give to the injured spouse. Some people will say you should leave, when they don't understand the loss. Some people will appear to lose respect if the injured spouse doesn't leave. This is not supportive or helpful. The injured spouse needs time to think clearly after the discovery, needs love and support. The injured spouse needs to make up his/her own mind. This is the only way healing can take place.

In my case my spouse wants to be with someone in the U.S. (we live in France) and he also wants to work there (which he has had a longing to do for some time). He goes to the U.S. regularly on holidays. Although he says he wants a divorce he still hasn't done anything about it yet, and he claims he does not want to marry this girl.

I wish there was some type of paper and pencil questionnaire that couples could fill out that would indicate the chances of repeated affairs in the future. My husband of 35 years betrayed me many times in the first 15 years (he was a philanderer), but then settled down for 16 years until 4 years ago when he began an affair with the bookkeeper at our business which culminated in the pair of them running off together. Three months later he did ask to return home, and after much communication, I did allow him back - he needed medical attention and felt that I would be a better caretaker. Now, he says that he really wants to rebuild the marriage. I don't know whether to believe him or not. He has lied so much. Wish I had left him during the early years of our marriage - much grief could have been avoided. If there had been a test or some indicator of what lay ahead way back then, perhaps I could have summoned the courage to leave.

The verbal and emotional abuse was getting worse and a couple of times physical abuse. My husband now is living with his other woman, but is at our home each morning before work and on weekends, helping to do things. I can see a change in both of us and I have high hopes that our marriage will survive. I think he's beginning to find that "the grass is not greener" after all. I know in my heart that he's having a midlife crisis; there are so many other things involved; hating his job, feeling it's his turn to have fun, sick of responsibility, drinking, starting to smoke after quitting 10 years ago, hanging out with younger people (his girlfriend is 14 years younger).

My husband is living with the affaire and is seeking a divorce. I do not want the divorce and seek a reconciliation. Married 17 years...he was involved in affair only several months before wanting divorce. She is 25 (15 years younger), divorced her second husband to be with him and has an 8-year old son from her first marriage. Have yet to meet anyone who believes this will last. I believe this is his only affair...I suffered from undiagnosed chronic depression (now on medication - doing extremely well). I truly believe he cannot forgive himself for this...he has all but said so to me. Hope we can at some time reconcile this marriage. His father has cheated many times over (never left), both his sisters have cheated and divorced. Runs in the family?

Separating

I am currently still married. Have been separated for two years. He moved in with his girlfriend in one week after I moved out. I filled out divorce papers but never filed due to him being retired military and me receiving those medical benefits. I have not seen him but one time in two years.

My husband and I separated after he assured me he would not see her anymore but did. After I left him and moved 350 miles away, he finally stopped seeing her and came to visit us every weekend, and he asked that we start dating again, gradually asked me to move back home, and after some time I moved back with our kids. I believe that he will never cheat on me again; however, sometimes I do feel uncomfortable with the fact that he did betray me...he emotionally shared himself with this person.

There may have been two "affairs"...one that caused my wife to leave (separated/she filed for divorce). After leaving, she and others mention a boyfriend where she lives in another state. I clearly will forgive and will devote myself to our well-being and future together. We have 35 good years behind us and possibly that many ahead of us. I see my wife as my best friend, my angel. All of this is only gut level presumption based on all else that I saw, heard and sensed.

When I attempted to discuss this with my wife I was met with a barrage of anger, denial, and meanness. I wanted to hear, "I love you, please forgive me and let us work together to resolve this and move forward, together." I did not accuse, but I did breach the subject. I just wanted the relationship over and to go on with our lives. Since that time my wife said one day," I don't love you, I've never loved you, I've never been in love with you, I'm leaving you, don't try to stop me, I'm leaving, if you try to find me I will hide and you will never see me again. I told my Dad on the morning he was to marry us that I didn't love you and that I did not want to marry you. I married you on the rebound, I never loved you, and I've never been in love with you, I'm leaving you!" She moved 2100 miles away 5 months ago. We have had about 5 hours of conversation on the phone (reluctantly and with anger on her part) and I was able to see her for one hour when she was in our town for 8 days. She is my wife. I love her, no matter what. I will not forsake her. I will not sin against her. I will wait on her. I will pray for her daily. The possibility of the affair and then a boyfriend was not the issue for me; it was about losing her, the death of our relationship, which I am willing to reconcile. People say I have changed so much since she left, that I am a different and better man. I am not so sure about the change as I am about knowing that I understand now. I understand all that was in our marriage that brought us to the point of another person and then separation. I know that I would never settle for that life again, for the pain I put upon her, and the anger that it created in her. I was a workaholic, and she felt so left out. Now she is out of her home and away from her family, in pain and very, very angry toward me. She is also afraid of me, and certainly not because of me, perhaps because of my past convictions about a monogamous relationship. She will not communicate with me. When I saw her last she said I was to have no further communication with her. I asked her if during that time (of the possible relationship) if she felt as though it was none of my business because she no longer cared about me, and she answered, "yes, that's right." My life is moving forward as much as possible now, and I have grown because of this. My only hope is that she finds it in her heart to love me again, so that I may love her as unconditionally and caring as possible for this man. Now I have a broken heart, and facing the pain of reconciliation and reconstruction will be far less than the pain from the forever loss of a best friend, an angel, a spouse.

It's been a year since I decided to give him a second chance at staying married. It started out great but has digressed for me into a daily painful experience. We separated to discover "you don't know what you have till it's gone," but later learned he wanted me out so he could focus on her. To this day I know I am gutless - I should have left him, but I did try going through a divorce and panicked, ran back to him, and have been with him since. I'm not independent. I don't have a strong sense of self-esteem. I am to begin counseling tomorrow on my self-image, but I'm so confused about trust and lies and "what if's."

Friends and relatives are helpful at first in the separation event. They love and support you as best they can. After awhile, however, you need more help and unless they have been through a similar situation, are unable to really understand.

Divorce

In my case, I have just decided to divorce since my wife cannot completely guarantee that she will refrain from having contact with this individual (she claims to just be friends now - I'm more than skeptical about that). The individual who has had the affair should give up all contact with their lover, including gifts and mementos; this cannot be emphasized enough. While it is true that there were a number of things that need to be worked on by both the parties in this marriage, it was her inability to "puke him up" and get him worlds away from our lives as rapidly as possible that put an insurmountable psychological barrier in the way. Staying married after an affair is a difficult enough proposition even if the person who had the affair ends all contact with their outside lover. It's seemingly impossible if they don't.

He left the very night he told me and moved in with her. She is now divorcing her husband too. He does not see the kids because he does not want to make his girlfriend mad. I just started the divorce recently. We are not divorced yet.

Husband has NOT stopped seeing other woman. We are separated. He says divorce, I don't want to. I believe he's reluctant to actually file since he hasn't done so yet (5 months).

Her affair was with my best friend, who I had asked to talk to her, as she was withdrawn and remote due to our son's drug problems. She revealed to him that 24 years before, shortly after we were married, she had been raped by her employer, and never told a soul. I went through with a divorce after more than a year - due to her unwillingness to admit her feelings of love for my friend (he's married, but she refused to stop contacting him) and to face the consequences of her rape and her affair in our lives. She simply wished to stop talking and go forward. I couldn't.

I had to initiate the divorce because he was not paying child support after he left and moved in with the other party in the affair. To get any help, I needed to initiate the divorce. He had no desire to get one, living the way he was, was fine with him, but this was not the way that I could continue to live. He remarried 1 week after the divorce was final and according to our son, who is almost 18, the marriage is not at all happy and there is constant fighting. He is one unhappy man. I had rough times, but have decided that I am better off now than I was then.

My spouse refused to sever all ties or contact with the person she had the affair with. She eventually returned to this same person a year later, but denied that she did. The reason for her wanting a divorce was that she did not love me anymore (as a wife) or that we were "incompatible." I have always desired reconciliation and honest communication, even in the immediate aftermath of the discovery of the initial affair. She still denies that a second affair with this same person took place. She simply felt it necessary to obtain a divorce, which I eventually agreed to, only for the sake of ultimately reconciling with her. I know the above sounds strange, but it is the truth as I see it. Even after being divorced one year, she is willing to at least "keep the door open" to reconciliation for three reasons, she maintains: 1) all the years we were together; 2) the children (we have four); 3) she still "cares for me." Our relationship is cordial, friendly, based on mutual parenting of our children, and I pray that reconciliation might some day occur.

Divorce is the most painful thing I have ever experienced.

I was thrown totally for a loop...I am going on with my life but still get very sad and tearful. I am not afraid of a new relationship but have not really tried to get into any settings for one. Very painful during a very painful time. Very difficult to go through at 50! I am positive and improving, Am looking forward to some sort of relationship...but not looking for one really.

I don't know if I still have the facts related to what happened. He told me the moment he was involved in an affair (the next day, by phone since he was out of town), and I knew something was happening by his voice, etc. He announced immediately the marriage was over and there was no discussion or joint counseling.

My now ex-husband left me with a one-month old daughter; he left us with no source of income, and he took the car. To make matters worse he left me for a teenager. I was so angry. My family rallied around me. They sent my daughter and me to California to visit my sister. It was there that I began to come to terms with everything. I live in a rural community and needed to be away from the gossip and I needed to focus my attention on my daughter and healing myself. A little over a year has passed since he walked out. I find that I am a happier person now than I was at any point in our relationship. Through counseling I learned how to address my anger and let it all out. I feel at peace, and happy. I have met a new man and I am taking it all one step at a time. I guess I just want to tell others in my situation it is ok to be angry, get mad. Confronting all the anger helped me to get beyond it and be the mother and person that I want to be.

I feel divorced, since she openly is with this person, has introduced this man to my daughter, we have joint legal and physical custody (50-50), she filed for divorce (going to trial) and financially manipulated as I thought we were cooling off and working it out while she was talking to lawyers. She not only is unregretful but is bullying me financially and emotionally.

We'd been married about six years. After that, we stayed together and he continued to have affairs...he was a clergyperson, and had affairs with women in every church in which he served, sometimes more than one, until he finally got caught by the powers-that-be. We divorced after 21 years of marriage, and 8 affairs that I know of.

At the time of the divorce, our child was a toddler and has multiple handicaps. Since the divorce I have cared for the child on my own, worked full time, and remained completely celibate. My parents help out when they can. Child support comes intermittently, without any attending interest in the child's welfare or progress.

My divorce has been so devastating to me that even after 18 months of him meeting his new young thing, I still have days where I just don't want to get out of bed.

I did not want to get the divorce, however there is no-fault divorce in our state. Basically, my spouse didn't need my approval despite the fact that we had 3 children under the age of 6. I am healed and have actually improved my life, but I would still not want to divorce my spouse that quickly.

In my situation, getting a divorce from my ex-husband was the only sensible thing to do. The affair was only a final straw in a long list of things that went wrong in the marriage from day one. While receiving therapy, I discovered that after 14 years of divorce some of those issues still haunted me. Getting the divorce improved me as a person; it allowed me to take charge of my life and not to depend on anyone. Yes, this causes for a lot of loneliness. I have actually avoided developing relationships so that I don't have to deal with any more disappointments.

I have been divorced since July of 1996 and am on my own and I LOVE it! I have had several dates and romances as I traversed the early part of being divorced. I am now seeing one man exclusively.

Divorce does not have to be the outcome of an affair, but in my experience, I was not given any other choice. My ex was the person to make the decision to divorce. I'm not entirely sure if we could have overcome her affair. I strongly recognize that both parties must devote themselves to recovery in all phases and with all the resources available to create the opportunity for the marriage to survive. In my case, no effort from my former wife was given toward any reconciliation. She told me she wanted a divorce and left permanently within hours of my discovery.

I believe my spouse carries extreme denial of any hurt that he has caused. He feels that because he was unhappy in our marriage (because of responsibilities and my criticisms) he was "justified" in leaving the marriage. He claims "the other woman" was not a determining factor in his decision to leave. But she does "make him happy."

At present, my husband and I are still married, but in the process of a divorce. He told me that he loved me and our children, but could not live with us with the feelings of guilt and unworthiness that he felt. I have forgiven him and I still love him, but he refuses to come home (separated for 4 months) and "Live A Lie." I have begged for him to explain what that means and he says that this is all about him and not a slap at his family. I beg to differ because his actions did and continue to have great effects on his family.

Former spouse decided on divorce before I learned of affair, which had been taking place for at least a month. Third party was an ex-boyfriend from high school and college. Would not discuss counseling.

A couple of weeks after we decided to work it out my husband went back to the other woman. I did not know this until almost a year later. When I discovered it he said he wanted a divorce and filed for one and moved in with other woman. I was very upset and didn't want him to leave, which has caused him some grief because now he is thinking of coming back. He did not expect the reaction he got from me that I want him back. An important thing about why he started this affair in the first place was that he assumed I was cheating on him, which was not true at all. This affair started from the Internet.

My wife had two affairs (one I knew about) and it was ok with me. We would have gotten divorced ether way, the affairs had nothing to do with it. (I had many affairs, but she never knew about them.)

She had 4 affairs all together, the last two were online, she drove 3,000 miles sight unseen to her last online lover in California. The fact that she would never admit to any of the adultery until faced with irrefutable proof leads me to believe there was more. We reconciled after the first two affairs (happened at the same time) and things were good for four years till the Internet.

To me, you work out things first, then arrive at whether or not divorce is necessary or not. Also, "Family is everything" and nothing should destroy a family. That's how I feel. We are still married pending the divorce trial coming up in a few weeks. I don't have a problem with working everything out to save our family, she does. I can forgive her for the past, but I won't forgive her ever for destroying our family.

Staying married

I still wonder if I made the right decision to stay with him, and fear that he will stray again if put under too much stress by me and my teenagers. It is hard to trust again, but one good thing did come out of my husbands infidelity...I got myself a job, am now more independent, and am able to make clearer decisions. Who knows if the pain won't tear us apart one day!!!!!

I am having trouble understanding why I stay in the marriage when I recently learned that my husband just had another affair and insists he was trying to rebuild our marriage at the same time. So many lies....so much deception....so many secrets....all my attempts at honesty were diverted by him or dismissed as my "craziness."

I am moving on with my husband and my married life but I have been FOREVER CHANGED from this event. I trusted too easily, believed too much in the happy ever after...I believed in the "goodness of people" and that for the most part people who say they love you in fact do love you. My belief system has changed dramatically...I am more cynical more careful about who and what I believe...I will never again ignore or question my instincts. I recognize my own personal standards of conduct and level of honesty is higher than most...even that of my spouse...this was a shock to me. Now I know love takes hard work and time and continued nourishing and open and honest communication. I also want to say that my marriage before the affair was not a bad marriage; I had many happy years with my husband. We had a good marriage before the affair in many ways...that's one of the key reasons why I decide to stay and work on saving the marriage and the relationship.

I feel he was having a "midlife crisis." He feels like he is hurting as much as I am, but I don't know how he could. I never thought we would be here, he never felt it would happen either. We are pretty much committed to saving our marriage, but it will never be the same.

My wife told me about her affair during our first year of marriage. She told me 6 months ago after 5 years of marriage. Through counsel with our pastor and prayer and having all my questions answered, we have been able to get through this and build a stronger marriage, more than I thought was possible. I am thankful that my wife loved me enough to tell me about this and not have to carry the burden of hiding the past anymore with this heavy burden, and I forgave her right after she told me.

I think to get through it, the couple needs to be able to talk about it. The wife has to be able to trust the husband again, and the husband has to work to prove his trustworthiness. I also believe that for a relationship to survive infidelity, the couple needs to be together longer than just a year, as we were.

My husband is still involved with the woman to the point she thinks he is totally hers. We are still married, but I no longer sleep with him. But we are friends to a point. And foolish person I am, I still believe that one day it will be just us again. I still love him and could put this all behind me if he would just leave her. I believe he does love her but can't let me go either. This has lasted 5 years now.

In my case, being male, my main fear is that my wife will forever compare me with the other man. It is also very important that husband, victim or infidel, take an aggressive role in building up the wife. I have learned to pursue my wife so that she knows that she is number one in my life. My best friend cheated on his wife and never really pursued her and she still suffers after 5 years.

How the person who had the affair acts afterwards is crucial. I am lucky to have a husband who is deeply sorry for his poor choice for problem-solving. I think personal integrity has much to do with long-term resolution. Admitting errors in big issues does not come easy for either side, but once you do there are solutions. Tough as it is to go through, we are learning the impact of our love for each other and our family. It's strong and healthy, not perfect by any means. I have days of sadness, he has days of remorse. We talk and hug and speak sincerely. All we can do sometimes is just hold each other and cry or smile. His love for me is clear; life is chances to grow at different levels, at different times. We're still growing and hanging in there every day.

Living through my husband's affair has been a life-altering experience. However, I do believe that we are closer than we have ever been in our 17 years of being together. This year we're celebrating our 15th anniversary and for that, and the sake of our children, I am grateful. I do think of the mistrust often and I am trying to work through that, but it has changed me as an individual also. Knowing that I deserve better than what I was dealt and if I am not happy, I won't stay in this relationship. To report to date....I (we) are very happy and have had a greater love than we have ever had.

I am not happy that this affair happened at all, but it has helped our marriage tremendously. We both realized what we almost lost, and our marriage has grown stronger and better than ever before.

I wonder if I've done the right thing for my 9-year old son and myself by staying. At this point I still can't fathom making peace within myself.

My husband's first affair began within six months of our marriage and left me confused, hurt, and humiliated. We had no children, but I chose to stay with him. I discovered a subsequent affair when my husband gave me a venereal disease. At this time I had a two-year old son and no means of support. I did not confront him because I was afraid to be alone with my son. I wanted my son to have a father. However, it was at this point in my marriage that I threw in the towel on my marriage. It is now 23 years later and I am still married to this man and had a second son who is now 14 years old. The second child was unplanned, but loved nonetheless. I've continued on in this marriage for the second son. I only have 4 more years to go. The marriage has deteriorated so badly that I doubt that this is a healthy situation for my young son. I may not make the last 4 years. Am I crazy?

I stayed married because of my child. I lost all of my feelings for my spouse five years ago.

The hurt partner must honestly examine the character of the cheating partner. Will that person change? Not, are they willing to change. When affairs are exposed the cheating partner is willing to do anything to save a marriage. Then go right back to doing the same thing. What is most important, is that person capable of changing? What is their nature?

If you truly love someone, the scars from an affair never go away. There will always be someone or something that will be a constant reminder of your mate's infidelity. My decision to stay was out of fear of making a wrong decision. So I made no decision. Until I feel strong enough to evaluate his attitude I will stay (where I am financially secure) until my son leaves for college. If there are no more incidences until then, I will stay so that my son can be with his father.

Even though I would never want to go through this ever again (or in the first place for that matter), I am so thankful for how much closer we have grown through all of this.

Our love for one another was the main factor that made us decide to stay together.

Why did I decide to stay? We had been married 38 years and our history, business affairs and family are of high value to me. The good that came of this is that I identified what was important to me. Will I stay long term - Don't know! Have I gotten my affairs in order - Yes! Will I ever spend a day relaxed and not on guard again - Probably Not!

Although I'm still willing to "work" toward resolving the issues and trying to rebuild the marriage, the future does not look good. In retrospect, the single biggest factor in our failure to rebuild the marriage was my spouse's failure to be honest with me at any point during the ordeal. In fact, she never really was honest with herself.

Staying together was based on love and forgiveness; each spouse must be willing to move on and to build each other up.

If this makes any sense, now that we've gone through it we both feel closer and feel as though our love has been tested and it survived the test.

We love each other very much and I am willing to work through his issues with him for the next several months. But there may come a time that we may have to go our separate ways if he can not make a further commitment to our marriage (i.e. have children). I still think about the affair from time to time.

I don't believe I chose to stay because I love him more than others love their spouses. I believe there are a lot of factors…children being a huge one. I also don't feel nearly as committed to the marriage as I did before.

Children

The affair resulted in a child. The only reason I stayed in the marriage is that my kids would have lost a father and that other kid would have gained one, and I must say he is a good father but a lousy husband.

Years ago my wife had an affair. Within the past few years we started having some problems with our oldest child (he is currently 17) and I have found out that he was a witness to some of the affairs.

I am not sure if we will remain married and did not want to involve the children until we have decided.

He tried to take our sons from me. We were in a custody battle for 9 months. He was successful in taking the boys (two of them, the older ones) moved them away from our home state to the state we were living in, (Wisconsin) where he had his sister, whom our sons barely knew, watching them. This lasted for several months. He then had his secretary, whom the boys did not know, move into our home, and she watched them. Besides that, I had our 6 year old son with me, and feared him finding me if I ever tried to do something to myself. My sons and I are reunited. We all went through family counseling.

In my situation, the affair started during the pregnancy of the child. Our child is now 3, and her father is still with the same other woman. We of course split up when the baby was 6 months.

I feel the need to talk to someone, but have not spoken to friends or family, to prevent the information from leaking out to our child. I do not want this to impact their father-child relationship, which is very important to our child.

My ex met her new man via the Internet. It was 1994, during a time of great stress (floods, fires, riots, etc.) and personal stress (earthquake damaged house, her mother became senile, car wreck), and she just up and bailed out. Wanted to take our son with her to where the new man lives. I lost everything else I had, but kept primary custody of my son. That is the one good decision I think I ever made.

My husband and I are both in individual and family counseling. My pre-teen daughter "discovered" the affair, which began on the Internet.

I think I couldn't contain it. After she has stopped for awhile, the affair continued with the previous guy and at the same time a new affair came into picture. After 22 years of marriage and 7 children between 7 and 21 (last year), my wife said she just wanted to enjoy intimate sex, which she hadn't had enough...just realized. To date we've been married for 23 years. Thinking about the future of our children, I decided now to let it be as long as it is being kept secret from the children and our family members.

I didn't tell our daughter until the last time when he got caught - because I was afraid she'd hear it publicly somehow. Interestingly, she didn't have a CLUE. The divorce completely blindsided her; she was 17 at the time.

Anger

After my suspicions were confirmed, my husband told me not to take it personally and that "Fidelity isn't important in a marriage." I am still full of rage.

My reaction of anger is appropriate and justified. His reaction to a healthy, happy marriage was self-destructive and selfish. He needs to grow as a man. I don't need to silence my anger as a wife who just became another statistic.

After 2 1/2 years I am just now getting over some of the anger, but it has only been after constant assurances of my husband's regret for the affair and, more importantly, his assurance that he didn't love her. He treats me better than he ever has, and seems to have undergone a personality change for the better.

I feel strongly that by becoming self-sufficient in providing for myself and my children, my fear of abandonment will not overwhelm me and will allow me to retain self-respect when this happens again. (I'm quite certain it will.) It's how he "handles" his own feelings of inadequacy; e.g. too much stress at work, financial difficulties that can't be easily resolved, etc. I feel it's up to me to be my own protector and in that way make my husband understand I will not be his scapegoat again. We've been married 21 years and have only recently been able to have children. He's had at least seven other "emotional attachments" (doesn't admit to sexual encounters) during that time, the first in our first year of marriage! He feels I'm too possessive - I'm learning to remove that prop of an excuse. Lots of anger here!! I found out about the second affair yesterday, and I don't understand why there isn't anyplace to turn to for displaced wives and children. I had to leave my home (it's his family home) and stay with a friend without my children. Now I risk him trying to take custody of them while I'm trying to find a place to go with my children. If I had been battered I could go to a shelter, but instead I've just been betrayed and my family taken from me. I now have 3 options. Leave him and take the kids, leave the kids with him, or go back to him and know that this is going to happen again. We need someplace for people like me to turn to.

My wife was a model for 10 years. During her career she had relationships with many "famous" men. The affair was with a multi-millionaire, former professional basketball player. She was cruel and seemed angry with me during the time of the affair. We have a 2-year old daughter. When the affair began, our daughter was around 1 year old. She would leave our daughter with me, or day-care and be with her "other partner." I don't believe she is in contact with this person. However, she maintains contact with other men from her past. I'm a strong person. But, this has left me wounded and angry.

Talking

My husband never openly gave me information. When I found out, I had to fight for our marriage and he seemed to enjoy that. When I made the decision to be strong and move on and it showed, he all of a sudden became interested in our marriage. I have asked many times (too many to count) for the truth, but we always end up in a fight because he refuses to tell me anything I don't already know. When I push for information he gets defensive and nothing is resolved. He always accuses me of bringing up the past, which for me is still the present because he has never given me the information I need to heal. It has been over a year since the affairs (many online affairs), and I am still asking for information. We will not survive if he refuses to be honest. I think I have come to a point where I will not ask anymore and if we don't make it, then we don't, but I am tired of trying.

We tried many different ways to put this behind us; the only way it began to work was when I was ready to forgive and when my wife was ready to tell the whole truth and answer all my many questions honestly! It's been 11 years now and my wife and I are very happy together. I trust she will never again do this to us. And I know I have no interest in having an affair. It's not worth the PAIN!

We were high school sweethearts and have been married for forty years. My wife had a three-year-long affair with her boss during our second through fourth years of marriage. She was nineteen when it started. She told me a little about it three years afterward. However, she only said that they had frequent sex and that she had been the one to cut it off. I desperately wanted all the details. She would say nothing more. I felt that, given time, she would be willing to tell me all. However, in thirty-five years, she still refuses to do so. I am obsessed with the need to know. When I brought it up recently she said, "Let go of it! I was a naive nineteen-year-old and didn't know better!" What should I do?

It takes a lot of work to stay together after an affair. And it has to be important to both parties involved. For me the only lingering thing is that I don't know any details. He told me he did not feel right talking about it, and I try to respect that, but it is not easy.

It was almost 1 1/2 years ago that my husband had his affair. I know very little about it. He refused to talk about it--said it was over and done. I still hurt today. I don't even know for sure that he is still not seeing her. I just wish the pain would go away and that I could forget all about it. So afraid that it could happen again.

We only make progress if I don't talk about it. If I bring up "us," not necessarily the affair, she tends to clam up or say, "I thought we were doing ok..." I just want to know if she really loves me AND is attracted to me, or if she is just "trying" to love me until this whole thing blows over - so that her family and co-workers don't find out what she did (everyone thinks she is an angel).

When I found out I wanted to know so many details. He refused to tell me all but some, which I now think was for the best. But, I must admit, there are times I wish I knew more. This was a point I was extremely caught up on, and one which I think many people involved in similar situations have trouble with.

My husband "does not want to hurt me," so does not want to discuss his affair. I think when I bring it up it makes him feel guilty. I don't know if I will ever get over it.

We have talked quite a bit about the affair but I have had to drag the details from her. This has delayed our recovery and closure. Because it was difficult to get answers from her, I still wonder whether she was truthful and told the whole truth. It is taking longer for me to rebuild trust.

I can forgive him of the infidelities if he would just talk to me. I still feel much bitterness and anger because of this situation.

My husband had a very long term affair (5.5) years. It was on and off with a lot of lying to me. It's been 6 months since it ended and it's still very painful for me. Mostly, because he won't talk about it and doesn't want to hear about what he was like and how he treated me. He claims he doesn't recall any of the behavior I describe.

It was very important that my husband answer honestly all of my questions, even if the answers hurt at the time. In that way, I knew he was being honest with me, not just telling me what I wanted to hear.

As the spouse of someone who had an affair it was absolutely key that my husband told me everything I wanted to know...this was not easy and took a long time to get through...well over a year. Also key was his support and willingness to hang in with me while I grieved and my emotions ran the gamut of disbelief to anger to rage to plain old complete sadness. I quite often said to him if this is too much for you to deal with, feel free to leave...I even encouraged him to leave because I simply could not "fake" feeling better when I did not and I did not want to feel guilty about being down. He consistently said he wanted to be there and wanted to be at home and that he was sorry and that he was responsible for me being in the place I was. It is now 18 months past discovery and it is getting easier but I still slide and grieve what I cannot change about my past, but I can see a light now that was not there at the point of discovery. Yes, recovery is possible but not without a lot of hard painful work and the ability to withstand all the grueling emotions. I would guess at this point that real recovery emotionally takes probably upwards of five years. An affair I believe is probably the single most devastating event that can impact on a marriage and the relationship between the two parties in that marriage. The vows that are broken, although they can be repaired, will forever be changed.

The lack of details about the affair, answers about the deceit to cover it up, and the decision to let the affair ultimately destroy our marriage and family has not been openly discussed and I may never find closure and resolution for myself. That is the saddest part for me, because the reasons for and answers about the affair have only been discussed, briefly. I truly want and need to have the answers so my emotional peace might be found again. Without answers, I continue to question myself and I cannot heal the wounds completely. My ex has the information but continues to withhold it. One of the hardest realities for me is understanding and accepting that she's now engaged to be married to the third party, which does not happen too often, according to the statistics. In retrospect, I will candidly admit that this entire experience has and continues to be the most painful and destructive period in my life, both emotionally and physically. I'll carry these deep scars for forever.

I have found that the willingness to discuss an affair seems to be an indicator of the willingness to recommit to the marriage. I found out about the affair "during," not "after" the affair, but my wife was unwilling to talk about it until the affair was truly over (about two months later). The number of "encounters" were few (three).

I just discovered, almost two months ago. The affair lasted for 1.5 month according to him. I'm still in pain, resentment because of his lack of communication. He doesn't want to answer all my questions.

Once an affair is discovered I believe all nitty-gritty details should be confessed, feelings, activities, duration, etc.

My wife and I are only a few weeks into working the situation through. The largest stumbling block seems to be the difficulty she faces in resolving her feelings about her affair. She does not want to analyze it much or admit a fantasy motivation because that would, I think, lower the high plane that she thought the relationship was on (twin souls, star-crossed lovers, etc). It might also lower her opinion of herself if it becomes "just a common affair" that she acted upon. I cannot begin to rebuild a new relationship with her until I have a stable base to build it on. I need the affair to be resolved before I can move on. I am very understanding but don't know how to help her.

Our marriage is like a cup whose handle has been broken off and glued back together. While it's still functional, it will never be as strong as the original item. My spouse denied the affair as just a "friend" thing even though I know better and refused to talk about it at all, leaving me to cope with all the issues by myself, which leads to thinking the worst of the situation.

I believe that my husband's unwillingness to discuss his affair has hampered our "recovery." How can I ever trust him again if I feel he is still being deceptive and not being totally candid and open about what caused the affair, how serious it was, etc. etc.?

Honesty/Lying

My husband lied to me incessantly about his affair and still does. I can't seem to get the truth; he's like two people with two stories at the same time. It's been just a little over a year now, I have never been allowed any closure or healing, it's all been about my husband.

When I first discovered his affair, she had broken up with him because she found out that he was married. He wasn't sure what he wanted to do. I wanted to see if we could improve our relationship, as divorce is not something I want if possible to prevent. After a few weeks he decided that he also wanted to work on us. However, after knowing, I became wiser to clues and listened to my intuition. I found that in spite of his claims, he had taken up with her again, while denying it to me. I finally told him that I knew and wasn't going to accept the lies. I felt by then he had ended it again and he seems to be more committed to try. It's harder for me because of that backsliding. But there have been improvements in our relationship and I hope we can come out of this in a better way. He is a good man and has many positive qualities, or I don't think I could go through this pain.

I never saw it coming, and I never suspected she had been having this affair for years. I think of myself as a very loving and caring person. I wanted to know how my wife's life was and cared about her opinions and cares, but she could look me straight in the eye and lie through her teeth and I never suspected a thing. She still to this day will tell me "nothing sexual has ever gone on between me and him or me and anyone else" even though I know this is a lie. My biggest question is why is she still lying about it? We're divorced, she's been living with him, she has told the rest of her family that they are intimate, but why does she insist on lying to me?

My husband refused to address the problems which arose through his infidelity, thereby creating a continuing scenario of rejection. He has rejected me for eight years without explanation. Recently the woman with whom he had an affair called my home to talk to me. Although this caused more hurt, it may have opened the doors for the marriage to heal. I frequently told my husband that it was not the affair but his treatment of me when he came home that did the most damage. After his affair mate called, I told him that understanding and support of his crisis had done nothing but damage our relationship. The last eight years were not wasted as we raised our children, but personally it was a very damaging situation for me and for him. His lack of courage to face what he did and his inability to be honest with me caused more harm than the affair itself. Honesty and trust is what counts. Those are better arms of comfort than any other.

111

My first husband had an affair. I am now engaged to be married to a wonderful man. The only thing is that even though he has never done anything for me to even suspect him of any of this type of behavior, I still sometimes find myself being scared that it might happen again. We talk about it a lot and are very open about what the affair did to me and what it did to my first marriage. He is willing to be open about everything he feels about me, about other women in life and his life. I never experienced that type of honesty before. It makes me feel secure in a way that I have never known.

It wasn't the affair as much as the lying.

I do feel a marriage can make it, but only if that person who has the affair is honest all the time with you, wanting to prove to the person how much he wants it to work. It is lots of hard work and there is no guarantee it will last. I felt that if my husband and myself would have communicated more a long time ago, just maybe this could have been avoided.

I feel that honesty and complete truth of the affair has to be given nowadays when we are dealing with AIDS, etc. It would be easier to deal with the topic if you know complete facts than always questioning the action. Then you could let go easier instead of waking up dreaming about issues and always wondering.

How or when can you ever believe a spouse when he/she says there were no feelings attached to the affair, or it was an ugly situation? There were nothing but lies when the affair was happening, why should I believe these things that I'm being told now?

My husband made it all worse by trying to hide it for months and each lie built. His health has suffered through the stress also, as he has had stress-induced heart problems since. I am still angry. I understand a lot of the situation, but the trust is hard to rebuild. His actions throughout the past five years of our 15-year marriage have helped rebuild the marriage (this happened last year and was made known to me in January of this year). But still...it's hard to shake the depression and major sense of loss.

I can't seem to forgive him all of the terrible things he has done. Especially the lies! I feel he should have been honest with me from the very beginning and given me the chance to know exactly why our marriage was suffering so. I couldn't understand what the problem was.... now I know.

I believe the affair is still going on and I found proof that he's lying to me.

I cannot emphasize communication and honesty enough. It occurs to me, though, that not everyone is interested in being honest or maintaining a commitment, for whatever reason. I've been in a fair amount of relationships in my life, and thought that I could "read" my partner pretty well. But I didn't see it coming.

Trust

I can't imagine trusting someone like that again, and the affair pretty much destroyed whatever ideals I had about romance. Maybe later I'll decide that it was necessary for growth, and I'll be able to appreciate a "real" relationship. But I doubt it.

Still have trouble trusting completely. In a relationship now where things are going good, but I'm nervous and think I'm looking for things to be wrong so I can break it off. Very hesitant in growing close to someone.

We're trying to build the trust, but it's a long, painful journey that I thought we'd never have to go though. I'm still hurting.

I still feel very threatened by the loss of trust and doubt very much that the level of trust can be re-established.

My spouse believes that since she has voluntarily told me of these affairs that all is well and she should be trusted.

I trusted him completely and had put him on a pedestal. Thought he loved me only and would never hurt me, but he did. Now I want to die for being so stupid. He had a fantasy, got obsessed about it and decided to live it up without putting my feelings in perspective. Basically he took advantage of my trust and innocence to do something he says he's ashamed of, but I have lost my trust in him now. I still have special affection for him, but my love is not the same anymore. He says he's going to work on getting where we were before, but how can I work on it. I feel that he did not respect me before enough to control himself, why should I think he respects me now, even though he keeps telling me he does.

I doubt you can ever trust again. I believe you learn to live with the situation but you never regain the trust. Perhaps that's what makes your relationship deeper, you learn to express the feelings, concerns, and to ask questions, making it a relationship with more communication.

Knowing details helped me heal but also hurt. He had fun while I worked and cared for kids, etc. I was the good wife while he partied. I resent that. Now he says he appreciates me. Why not before? Having hard time trusting his words.

I have a great problem regaining trust. Also, I wish I knew how long this would take. I've worked so hard and after two years still feel discouraged. Frequently, I feel that it would have been more productive to put all this work into building a life filled with honesty on my own.

Wife had the affair. I feel that the lack of communication problems were the major factor in the affair. We are still married and living together. I have forgiven her for the affair. The trust is something that will come with time...I know that. She says that the affair happened only once. Have to believe to begin trust. I do.

I don't think I will ever trust him or believe him again.

I didn't think I would ever love again; but now I've met someone I love very much and he's restored my trust.

In my case, my husband continued having various affairs even while he was seemingly trying to help me "digest" his confession to his first two affairs, and while he was promising to "behave." This has seriously wounded my capacity for trust.

I will never trust him again. It ruined our church life; we were both very active in the church. It ruined our social life; friends left, only one female friend of mine remains a friend today. And it almost cost me my job.

I still do not trust my husband. I don't know that I ever will trust the way trust should be between a married couple. I feel that he blames me for part of the affair and that hurts me very much and makes me really angry.

This has been the most painful experience of my life. I know I will never forget it nor ever fully trust my husband again.

The issue of trust is the hardest to overcome as he travels every week. I can't dwell on it or I would go crazy. We both took our marriage very seriously, and when I confronted him and he admitted the affair I was devastated that he said it really was nothing, he was just trying to help out another co-worker who had too much to drink and she came on to him. I still blame him, as I am in the relationship with him not her.

Since my divorce, it's difficult to trust again so I don't have much of a dating social life. I'm enjoying discovering myself, healing even 5-1/2 years later and concentrating my focus on parenting my son. Someday I will love and be loved again, perhaps when I feel comfortable again and realize I have re-gained all I have lost.

Forgiving

I just want to go on with our future, I hate looking back, but I can't get past it. My husband is a great man, I really can't say why he had an affair, but I am positive that he will not do that again. Have I forgiven him? I feel like I have, but maybe not. It has been less than a year, and I still think about things I should have already buried.

It was not really an affair; it was more of a one-night stand. Although at the time I was very hurt and upset. I feel as though we have worked through this by overcoming this. It has made our marriage that much stronger. This is something that I honestly believe was truly a mistake and my wife is deeply sorry for it. This I cannot be a hundred percent sure of, but it will probably never happen again. If it were to happen a second time though, it will lead to a breakup. Once can be forgiven and worked out; more than that is disrespect for your spouse and lack of love in the relationship.

I am very concerned about the time it takes to overcome the fear and anxiety associated with an affair. How do I know if I've truly forgiven, or am I just going through the motions?

I can't forgive the affair, I do forgive that he hurt me, because he is sorry for the hurt. I feel we will go on together, but our marriage vows were broken and I have a problem with that; I'm not sure how to handle that part in my mind. Maybe like other things, I will deal with that. Time will tell.

I feel very strongly that I have stayed in this relationship because of the kids and because of financial reasons. I knew if I divorced my husband that my children's lifestyle would change and I didn't feel that they should be punished for something they were not a part of or had any control over. So I have had to live with the resentment of the situation my husband put our family in.

I have had no problem dealing with forgiving my husband. I feel a strong need for revenge on his ex-lover.

For me, the forgiveness needs to come to myself. How do I forgive myself? I blame myself for all the mishaps of our marriage. What did I not do to keep our relationship together? Was I too involved with the kids? School? My job? What didn't I give to him?

Personally Recovering

You never recover from it, not even if you love again, its the sense of betrayal...the lies…

My wife is now more communicative about the affair. This has helped. I am not as deep in the "pits" as I was, but sometimes the depression returns and visits for a day or two. She now seems to be genuinely sorry and often tells me so. Our marriage is improving, but it is taking me a long time to heal -- I've never been injured like this before.

Getting over an affair takes time; I feel it has to be at one's own pace. It would be nice if someone could give all the answers, but it doesn't happen that way.

I am having a very hard time recovering from this. At first I was going to divorce him and even filed with the courts. But after he begged me to come back, I realized I still loved him, and took him back. I dropped the divorce proceedings. I am still having a rough time of it. I don't trust him like I used to and feel that I will never really recover from this betrayal.

I completely forgive my husband and he has been wonderful at trying to do all he can for me but I just can't forget those horrible details that I just had to know. They will always be in my head and I don't know if we'll stay married or not. It's been a year and I still sob daily.

I feel that now after I though I was over it (6 years have gone by), I've started feeling haunted by it again. I'm becoming extremely jealous and suspicious, though in my more intelligent moments, I can look at it from a different perspective and see that I have no reason to be. I'm suddenly struggling again, and my husband does not understand why, after all this time, it's suddenly an issue again. He feels hurt that I'm suddenly questioning his comings and goings, and I'm afraid of what this is doing to us now.

I'm trying to focus on giving myself the "gift" of letting it all go. While very difficult, it does help. Knowing that we cannot change anything we do not acknowledge, I acknowledge the pain and am trying to let it go.

I still feel like I have some trouble letting go of the fact that he slept with someone else. It hurts very much knowing he was touching another women and that someone else was touching my husband. I do know that the affair is over, and our marriage is better now than ever, but that is still the one thing that still hurts very much, it has only been 3 and 1/2 months since it has ended and I am hoping to get that "mental picture" out of my head. Sometimes I will still cry over it when I'm alone.

I still have trouble when I see things that remind me of where they were together and the time that he was not there for me. I wish I could completely put it behind me, but I don't think that will ever happen.

I feel like I can't breath...

I remarried, and my new husband had an affair also; I got past it, however after 19 years of marriage, I never really got over it and we are now divorced because of his drinking problems. I then got involved with a married man (separated) who ended up leaving me to go back to first wife. He said he would always love me, but could not leave his wife, without "one more" good faith effort to resolve their problems. I am now alone and frustrated on this whole subject.

My husband had a very long affair - it lasted 7 of the nine years we've been married. I have to admit that our marriage is better even than before the affair. The odd thing is that it is in my thoughts almost constantly.

Betrayal is a very hard thing to deal with, and I'm not sure a person will ever be able to deal with it totally. It taught me a lot, but I wish I had never had to go through it.

It is difficult to imagine ever getting over an affair. Your feelings of betrayal and anger take many months to subside even a little. This is normal??? You have to keep remembering where you want to end up (together) and put up with the journey. One day you will get there.

One of the most important things my doctor told me during this time was to get outside and be in nature. This has helped me more than anything. Every time I started feeling down or sorry for myself I would take a walk.

I have been in a few relationships since my divorce in 1990. I seem to attract/be attracted to women who always seem to have other men "in the wings," which has left me an emotional wreck and completely untrusting anymore. No relationship has lasted more than a year and I'm always left for the "other guy" that had been lurking around.

Eventually I hope my wound will heal; after forty years it is a deep wound, one I never wished for and would never wish on another human being. I will survive and I am a loving person but I do not know if I will ever love so completely again. For that is how one gets destroyed. Deception names itself "Love" and in that guise lies, and therein lies a shattered heart.

It has been almost a year since my husband's affair ended and I have taken the time for myself to work through the pain and to examine my marriage relationship. I know why the affair happened and I've taken a good hard look at myself and I know the areas where I neglected the relationship. I feel I'm capable of digging in and working on the relationship, but I can't get past the betrayal and the mistrust. There's a bond that was broken and that's just not repairable.

It takes many months, even years, to heal the scars and strengthen the marriage to pre-affair status. I initially had hoped and expected a quick recovery.

My husband's affairs destroyed my self-esteem. It's taken me years of hard work, counseling, new friendships, and a very responsible new job to rebuild my confidence in myself. I had vowed to never get married again. After a few years, I met the man to whom I am now married - whose wife had had an affair. We talked ad-nauseum about trust before we finally got married. Now we trust each other completely. I'm so thankful. It could easily have gone the other way.

For a long time I blamed myself, but eventually came to realize that he was responsible for his own actions and I refused to be co-dependent. Sure, his actions hurt me immensely, but regardless, they were HIS actions, not my own.... and I can only be held liable for my own actions. It has taken me many years to come to this belief, and until I did, I never had another healthy relationship until my current marriage. My current spouse and I discuss everything, from attractions to others to our past experiences. I sincerely believe maturity and honesty are the keys to a healthy marriage, plus realizing that humans are very sexual "critters".

The affair was a 'wake up call' to myself...I am a worthwhile person who deserves and wants equality in my marital relationship...this I let slip. I realize I am stronger than I ever imagined but if I had a choice to learn all the things I have about myself as a result of my husband's affair 'awakening me,' I would still chose for it to have never happened because the heartbreak and loss of specialness is an intangible that will never be the same again... I do believe we will build a good life together and are, now that the affair is over, but recovering from a spouse's infidelity is like suffering a bad burn that scars... you can heal but you are never the same after...even if you have plastic surgery and the scars aren't visible, they are there underneath...you are changed forever.

Appendix I

Copy of Entire Questionnaire

RESEARCH QUESTIONNAIRE
Survey on Extramarital Affairs
By Peggy Vaughan

If you have ever had a spouse who had an extramarital affair...

We invite you to participate (anonymously) in this study. Our goals are to:
1) discover the factors that determine whether or not marriages are likely to survive,
2) determine the degree to which people are likely to personally recovery from this experience.

There are two parts to this questionnaire - which should take about 10 minutes to complete:
1) The basic demographic information needed to interpret the research data.
2) A list of 37 multiple-choice questions about your personal experience.

We realize that some of this information is very personal and sensitive, and it will be kept totally confidential. It will be used only for compiling a base of information to help people who are personally struggling with this issue - as well as to assist therapists in more effectively responding to those who seek their help.

Results will be published on the website after all responses have been collected and analyzed.
Since the usefulness of the data depends on having complete responses to all the questions,
only those questionnaires filled out in full can be included in this study.

Please note the required fields marked with an *

Demographic Information

Age: *

Under 20
20-29
30-39
40-49
50-59
60 and over

Appendix I

Year of Birth: *

Before 1940
1940-1949
1950-1959
1960-1969
1970-1980
Later than 1980

Gender: *

Male
Female

Current country/region of residence: *

USA
Canada
Mexico
Africa
Asia
Caribbean
Central America
Europe
Latin America
Mediterranean
Middle East
Pacific Rim
South America

Ethnic or Racial Group Membership: *

Hispanic: A person of Mexican, Puerto Rican, Cuban, Central or South American, or other Spanish or Portuguese culture or origin, regardless of race.

Help for Therapists

White, non-Hispanic Origin: A person having origins in any of the original peoples of Europe, North Africa, or the Middle East (excluding persons of Spanish or Portuguese origin).

Black (Afro-American, non-Hispanic Origin): A person having origins in any of the black racial groups of Africa (excluding persons of Spanish, Portuguese, Latin American, or other Hispanic origin).

American Indian or Alaskan Native: A person having origins in any of the original peoples of North America who maintains cultural identification through tribal affiliation or community recognition.

Asian or Pacific Islander: A person having origins in any of the original peoples of the Far East, Southeast Asia, the Indian subcontinent, or the Pacific Islands.

Religious Affiliation: *

Buddhism
Christianity/Catholicism
Christianity/Protestantism
Hinduism
Islam
Judaism
Other
None

Highest Level of Education Completed: *

Less than high school
Finished high school or equivalent
Some college
Two years of college
Finished four years of college
Some graduate education
Professional Degree (e.g., Law)
Master's Degree

Appendix I

Ph.D.
M.D.
Ed.D.

Current Personal Annual Income: *

Less than $10,000
Between $10,000 and 20,000
Between $20,000 and 40,000
Between $40,000 and 60,000
Between $60,000 and 80,000
Between $80,000 and 100,000
Between $100,000 and 150,000
Above $150,00

Your Occupation: *

Administrative Support (Including Clerical)
Construction Trades
Executive, Administrative, and Managerial
Full-time Homemaker
Handlers, Cleaners, Helpers, and Laborers
Marketing and Sales
Mechanics, Installers, and Repairers
Military/Armed Forces
Production
Professional and Technical
Service
Transportation and Material Moving
Other
Unemployed

Guidelines for Responding to Questions:

Answer all questions based on the FIRST marriage in which a spouse had an affair.

Answer all questions based on the first time you learned that an affair(s) took place.

Current status of marriage to spouse who had affair(s): *

Married and living with spouse
Married but not living together
Legally separated
Divorced
Widowed

Child (or children) with spouse who had affair(s): *

Yes
No

The Period During Courtship and Early Years of Marriage:

How long did you date your spouse prior to marriage? *
Less than a year
One to 5 years
More than 5 years

How did you (as a couple) deal with attractions to others? *
Were not attracted to others
Didn't discuss attractions
Talked openly about attractions

How did you as a couple deal with the issue of monogamy? *
Assumed monogamy without discussing it
Talked about it early in relationship, but did not continue to discuss it
Had ongoing discussions about our commitment to monogamy

The Period When the Affair(s) was Taking Place:

Did you suspect an affair? *
> Had no suspicions
> Had slight suspicion, but didn't focus on it
> Intensely suspicious

What was the primary factor that might have warranted suspicion? *
> Gut feeling/intuition that something was wrong
> Changes in spouse's attitudes and/or behavior
> Information I discovered or others told me

Did you confront your spouse about your suspicion? *
> No
> Yes, but in a somewhat tentative or casual way
> Yes, very strongly and/or persistently

The Discovery of the Affair(s):

How did you find out about the affair(s)? *
> Spouse voluntarily told me
> Someone else told me
> I "found out" on my own

How long ago did you find out? *
> Less than 1 year ago
> One to 5 years ago
> More than 5 years ago

How long had you been married when you found out? *
> Less than 5 years
> Five to 15 years
> More than 15 years

How long had the affair(s) been taking place when you found out? *
> Less than a year
> One to 5 years
> More than 5 years

How many affairs did you find out about? *
> One
> Two to 5
> More than 5

Talking about the Affairs(s) with Spouse:

How MUCH did you and your spouse discuss the whole situation? *
> Very little
> A good bit, but not as much as I wanted
> A lot

How LONG did the talking continue? *
> Less than 6 months
> Six months to 2 years
> More than 2 years

Was the talking helpful? *
> No, we just went over and over the same things
> Yes, but didn't resolve as much as I would like
> Yes, it was essential to my getting beyond this

Did you want to know details about the affair(s)? *
> No, I didn't want to know details
> Yes, but I wanted only general information (who, when, why)
> Yes, I wanted to know everything, including details

Did your spouse answer your questions? *
> No, refused to talk beyond basics
> Yes, but only told some of the information after much pressure
> Yes, told me everything I wanted to know

Talking about the Affair(s) with Others:

Who did you talk to? *
    No one
    Friends/family/others
    Professional (counselor/therapist/clergy, etc.)

How MUCH did you talk to friends/family/others (NOT including professionals)? *
    Not at all
    Very limited
    A LOT

Was it helpful to talk to friends/family/others? *
    Didn't talk or not useful
    Helped some, but not as much as I'd like
    Extremely helpful

Deciding Whether to Stay Married or Get a Divorce:

How long after discovery was there a decision as to whether to stay married or get a divorce? *
    Less than 3 months
    Three months to a year
    More than a year

What was the decision? *
    To stay married
    To get a divorce
    Still undecided

Your Current Condition (Regardless of Whether Still Married or Divorced):

Do you still dwell on the affair(s)? *
>   Yes, it's still a pain I carry every day
>   While I still think about it from time to time, it's not a constant focus
>   No, I've pretty much put it in perspective in my life and moved on

Do you feel a sense of forgiveness/resolution? *
>   No, I still have lots of anger and resentment toward my spouse (or ex-spouse)
>   I think I've "forgiven," but I don't feel it will ever be completely resolved
>   Yes, my spouse's behavior since ending the affair has allowed me to let it go

Have you healed? *
>   No, I'm still in great pain
>   I've healed somewhat but feel I will always carry a scar
>   I've mostly healed and actually grown in many ways

If you had Children:

Answer the next 2 questions ONLY if you had kids at the time you found out:

What were the ages of the kids when you learned of the affair(s)?
>   All under 6 years old
>   All between 6 and 13 years old
>   Various ages (including teenagers and grown kids)

What did you tell the kids about the affair(s)?
>   Didn't tell them
>   Told them, but only a very little
>   Told them most of the facts of the situation

Appendix I

If you Stayed Married:

Answer the next 2 questions ONLY if you stayed married:

Has trust been rebuilt?

    No, still very guarded

    Yes, but still somewhat cautious

    Yes, secure in trustworthiness at this point

Has the relationship "improved" compared to pre-affair days?

    No, the relationship is more distant and strained

    Not actual improvement, but about the same as before

    Yes, it's better than before the affair(s)

If you Got a Divorce:

Answer the next 3 questions ONLY if you got a divorce:

Who initiated the divorce?

    I did

    My spouse did

    It was a mutual decision

Have you been able to trust enough to develop another intimate relationship?

    No, I'm very anxious about ever being vulnerable to being hurt again

    I've developed another relationship, but "hold back" somewhat

    I've developed a new "trusting" intimate relationship

What is the quality of any new relationship?

    No new relationship

    Not as good as the early days of my previous marriage

    Better than any period of my previous marriage

If you had Counseling:

Answer the next 4 questions ONLY if you had some form of therapy/counseling:

How many counselors did you see?
>One
>Two
>Three or more

Answer the next 3 questions based ONLY on experience with "first" or "only" therapist/counselor:

Was the counselor helpful?
>No, mostly frustrating
>Yes, but not as much as I'd like
>Yes, very helpful

Did the counselor encourage honest communication about the affair(s)?
>No, encouraged us to quickly cover highlights, then move on
>Yes, but on a limited time frame and to a limited degree
>Yes, very supportive of ongoing honest discussions

Did the counselor focus directly on the issue of affairs?
>No, mainly focused on general marital problems
>Yes, but not as strongly or clearly as I'd like
>Yes, very directly dealt with this issue

Please be sure all required fields are completed in order for the form to be submitted. We appreciate your willingness to share your experience in order to help others.

(END OF APPENDIX I – COPY OF ORIGINAL QUESTIONNAIRE)

Appendix II

Complete Report of the Demographic Information

Demographic Information about Respondents

Age:

0%	Under 20
10%	20-29
35%	30-39
41%	40-49
12%	50-59
2%	60 and over

Year of Birth:

2%	Before 1940
14%	1940-1949
42%	1950-1959
34%	1960-1969
8%	1970-1980
0%	Later than 1980

Gender:

25%	Male
75%	Female

Current country/region of residence:

90%	USA
5%	Canada
0%	Mexico
0%	Africa
1%	Asia
0%	Caribbean
0%	Central America

1%	Europe
0%	Latin America
0%	Mediterranean
0%	Middle East
1%	Pacific Rim
0%	South America

Ethnic or Racial Group Membership:

4%	Hispanic:
91%	White, non-Hispanic Origin
3%	Black (Afro-American, non-Hispanic)
0%	American Indian or Alaskan Native:
2%	Asian or Pacific Islander:

Religious Affiliation:

0%	Buddhism
30%	Christianity/Catholicism
43%	Christianity/Protestantism
0%	Hinduism
0%	Islam
2%	Judaism
8%	Other
16%	None

Highest Level of Education Completed:

1%	Less than high school
13%	Finished high school or equivalent
21%	Some college
18%	Two years of college
21%	Finished four years of college
7%	Some graduate education
4%	Professional Degree (e.g., Law)
13%	Master's Degree

2%   Ph.D.
0%   M.D.
0%   Ed.D.

Current Personal Annual Income:
8%   Less than $10,000
8%   Between $10,000 and 20,000
31%   Between $20,000 and 40,000
23%   Between $40,000 and 60,000
14%   Between $60,000 and 80,000
6%   Between $80,000 and 100,000
7%   Between $100,000 and 150,000
3%   Above $150,000

Your Occupation:
14%   Administrative Support (Including Clerical)
2%   Construction Trades
14%   Executive, Administrative, and Managerial
12%   Full-time Homemaker
1%   Handlers, Cleaners, Helpers, and Laborers
5%   Marketing and Sales
1%   Mechanics, Installers, and Repairers
1%   Military/Armed Forces
1%   Production
33%   Professional and Technical
3%   Service
1%   Transportation and Material Moving
11%   Other
2%   Unemployed

(END OF APPENDIX II – COMPLETE REPORT OF THE DEMOGRAPHIC INFORMATION)

Appendix III

Responses Broken Down by Gender

Responses Broken Down by Gender
(Including notations of some key similarities and differences)

The Period During Courtship and Early Years of Marriage:

How long did you date your spouse prior to marriage? *

Men	Women	
22%	24%	Less than a year
68%	64%	One to 5 years
10%	12%	More than 5 years

How did you (as a couple) deal with attractions to others? *

Men	Women	
11%	16%	Were not attracted to others
70%	64%	Didn't discuss attractions
19%	21%	Talked openly about attractions

How did you as a couple deal with the issue of monogamy? *

Men	Women	
54%	48%	Assumed monogamy without discussing it
30%	32%	Talked about it early in relationship, but did not continue to discuss it
16%	20%	Had ongoing discussions about our commitment to monogamy

The Period When the Affair(s) was Taking Place:

Did you suspect an affair? *

Men	Women	
38%	31%	Had no suspicions
42%	43%	Had slight suspicion, but didn't focus on it
20%	26%	Intensely suspicious

What was the primary factor that might have warranted suspicion? *

Men	Women	
28%	34%	Gut feeling/intuition that something was wrong
46%	44%	Changes in spouse's attitudes and/or behavior
26%	22%	Information I discovered or others told me

Did you confront your spouse about your suspicion? *

Men	Women	
27%	22%	No
36%	35%	Yes, but in a somewhat tentative or casual way
37%	43%	Yes, very strongly and/or persistently

The Discovery of the Affair(s):

How did you find out about the affair(s)? *

Men	Women	Similarity: Both said about one-third of spouses voluntarily told
33%	33%	Spouse voluntarily told me
10%	16%	Someone else told me
57%	51%	I "found out" on my own

How long ago did you find out? *

Men	Women	
53%	46%	Less than 1 year ago
30%	40%	One to 5 years ago
17%	14%	More than 5 years ago

How long had you been married when you found out? *

Men	Women	
25%	22%	Less than 5 years
43%	38%	Five to 15 years
32%	40%	More than 15 years

How long had the affair(s) been taking place when you found out? *

Men	Women	
71%	68%	Less than a year
23%	24%	One to 5 years
6%	8%	More than 5 years

How many affairs did you find out about? *

Men	Women	
72%	67%	One
25%	26%	Two to 5
3%	6%	More than 5

Talking about the Affairs(s) with Spouse:

How MUCH did you and your spouse discuss the whole situation? *

Men	Women	
21%	20%	Very little
41%	39%	A good bit, but not as much as I wanted
38%	40%	A lot

How LONG did the talking continue? *

Men	Women	Difference: Women wanted/needed to talk longer
62%	53%	Less than 6 months
20%	36%	Six months to 2 years
8%	11%	More than 2 years

Was the talking helpful? *

Men	Women	Similarity: Both reported same difficulty in talking in a productive way
33%	32%	No, we just went over and over the same things
44%	45%	Yes, but didn't resolve as much as I would like
22%	23%	Yes, it was essential to my getting beyond this

Did you want to know details about the affair(s)? *

Men	Women	Similarity: Both overwhelmingly wanted details
6%	8%	No, I didn't want to know details
33%	30%	Yes, but I wanted only general information (who, when, why)
60%	62%	Yes, I wanted to know everything, including details

Did your spouse answer your questions? *

Men	Women	Similarity: Both had trouble getting spouses to talk
26%	28%	No, refused to talk beyond basics
54%	48%	Yes, but only told some of the information after much pressure
20%	24%	Yes, told me everything I wanted to know

Talking about the Affair(s) with Others:

Who did you talk to? *

Men	Women	Difference: Twice as many men talked to NO ONE
24%	11%	No one
43%	41%	Friends/family/others
33%	48%	Professional (counselor/therapist/clergy, etc.)

How MUCH did you talk to friends/family/others (NOT including professionals)? *

Men	Women	Difference: Almost twice as many men did not talk to friends/family
33%	18%	Not at all
41%	49%	Very limited
26%	33%	A LOT

Was it helpful to talk to friends/family/others? *

Men	Women	Difference: Once again, reflecting that men didn't talk
18%	9%	Didn't talk or not useful
45%	52%	Helped some, but not as much as I'd like
36%	39%	Extremely helpful

Deciding Whether to Stay Married or Get a Divorce:

How long after discovery was there a decision as to whether to stay married or get a divorce? *

Men	Women	
62%	55%	Less than 3 months
27%	30%	Three months to a year
11%	15%	More than a year

What was the decision? *

Men	Women	
52%	55%	To stay married
21%	19%	To get a divorce
28%	26%	Still undecided

Your Current Condition
(Regardless of Whether Still Married or Divorced):

Do you still dwell on the affair(s)? *

Men	Women	Similarity: Both still carrying the pain
56%	55%	Yes, it's still a pain I carry every day
30%	33%	While I still think about it from time to time, it's not a constant focus
14%	12%	No, I've pretty much put it in perspective in my life and moved on

Do you feel a sense of forgiveness/resolution? *

Men	Women	
29%	36%	No, I still have lots of anger and resentment toward spouse or ex-spouse
59%	54%	I think I've "forgiven," but I don't feel it will ever be completely resolved
12%	10%	Yes, spouse's behavior since ending the affair has allowed me to let it go

Have you healed? *

Men	Women	Similarity: Both having difficulty healing
30%	34%	No, I'm still in great pain
52%	48%	I've healed somewhat but feel I will always carry a scar
18%	18%	I've mostly healed and actually grown in many ways

Re: Children:
(The next 2 questions were answered ONLY by those who had kids with spouse.)

What were the ages of the kids when you learned of the affair(s)?

Men	Women	
56%	46%	All under 6 years old
24%	26%	All between 6 and 13 years old
20%	28%	Various ages (including teenagers and grown kids)

What did you tell the kids about the affair(s)?

Men	Women	
32%	27%	Didn't tell them
31%	32%	Told them, but only a very little
37%	41%	Told them most of the facts of the situation

Appendix III

Re: Staying Married:
(The next 2 questions were answered ONLY by those who stayed married.)

Has trust been rebuilt?

Men	Women	Similarity: Both having difficulty with trust
50%	54%	No, still very guarded
43%	41%	Yes, but still somewhat cautious
7%	5%	Yes, secure in trustworthiness at this point

Has the relationship "improved" compared to pre-affair days?

Men	Women	Similarity: Both show similar "improvement"
27%	24%	No, the relationship is more distant and strained
29%	31%	Not actual improvement, but about the same as before
44%	45%	Yes, it's better than before the affair(s)

Re: Getting a Divorce:
(The next 3 questions were answered ONLY by those who got a divorce.)

Who initiated the divorce?

Men	Women	Difference: Women initiate more divorces (with or without an affair)
41%	63%	I did
42%	27%	My spouse did
17%	10%	It was a mutual decision

Have you been able to trust enough to develop another intimate relationship?

Men	Women	
33%	44%	No, I'm very anxious about ever being vulnerable to being hurt again
37%	33%	I've developed another relationship, but "hold back" somewhat
30%	23%	I've developed a new "trusting" intimate relationship

What is the quality of any new relationship?

Men	Women	Difference: Twice as many men felt quality not as good as marriage
33%	42%	No new relationship
33%	17%	Not as good as the early days of my previous marriage
34%	41%	Better than any period of my previous marriage

Re: Counseling:
(The next 4 questions were answered ONLY by those who had therapy/counseling.)

How many counselors did you see?

Men	Women	
28%	26%	One
32%	24%	Two
40%	50%	Three or more

(The responses to the next 3 questions were based ONLY on experience with "first" or "only" therapist/counselor.)

Was the counselor helpful?

Men	Women	Difference: Men far more negative about helpfulness of counseling
77%	51%	No, mostly frustrating
15%	25%	Yes, but not as much as I'd like
8%	24%	Yes, very helpful

Did the counselor encourage honest communication about the affair(s)?

Men	Women	
24%	23%	No, encouraged us to quickly cover highlights, then move on
50%	44%	Yes, but on a limited time frame and to a limited degree
27%	33%	Yes, very supportive of ongoing honest discussions

Did the counselor focus directly on the issue of affairs?

Men	Women	
58%	59%	No, mainly focused on general marital problems
31%	27%	Yes, but not as strongly or clearly as I'd like
11%	14%	Yes, very directly dealt with this issue

About the Author

Peggy Vaughan is an internationally recognized expert in the area of extramarital affairs. Beginning with her first book in 1980, she has published many books about this issue, including her 1989 classic, *The Monogamy Myth,* and her most recent book on preventing affairs, *To Have and To Hold.*

Peggy's "societal perspective" of affairs has catapulted her into the forefront of the growing public discussion of this issue, where she is called upon to comment on the constant stream of news stories related to affairs. But it's her personal commitment to helping people recover from the emotional impact of a partner's affair that has gained her a worldwide following.

The primary arena for her ongoing work is her website (www.dearpeggy.com). Since 1996 the site has served as an Extramarital Affairs Resource Center for professionals and the public alike. It has several hundred pages of free information, including articles about affairs, a list of therapists who have been recommended as being effective in dealing with affairs, links to other sites, Peggy's reviews of books by other authors as well as a bookstore where she sells her own books.

Peggy has been married for fifty-five years, has two grown children and three grandchildren and makes her home in San Diego, California.

Other Books by Peggy Vaughan

The Monogamy Myth: A Personal Handbook for Recovering from Affairs
This is Peggy's 'classic' (first published in 1989, now in its third edition) containing an overview of the entire issue of affairs. It provides personal help in dealing with affairs as well as offering a societal perspective aimed at relieving the personal devastation of this experience.

To Have and To Hold: A Personal Handbook for Building a Strong Marriage and Preventing Affairs
This book, based on survey responses of 755 men and women, analyzes the difference between people's assumptions about how to prevent affairs vs. the actions and behaviors that actually work.

Dear Peggy: Peggy Vaughan answers questions about extramarital affairs
This Q&A book is made up of 260 questions and Peggy's responses. It includes issues of concern to the man or woman who had an affair, to the spouse hurt by an affair, and to the third party.

Musings on Life
This book contains 107 of Peggy's personal reflections on a wide range of life issues, including: relationships, integrity, communication, health, education, making a difference and being a woman.

The following books were co-authored with her husband, James Vaughan, Ph.D.

Beyond Affairs
This book was initially published in 1980 (and republished in 2010 with a 30-year update), telling the story of their personal experience in dealing with affairs during an earlier period in their marriage

Recovering From Affairs: A Handbook for Couples
This is a 39-page handbook based on a course the Vaughans developed and conducted for people recovering from affairs.

Making Love Stay: Everything You Ever Knew About Love but Forgot
This book shows couples how to transform their romantic love into a more permanent lasting love—avoiding the gimmicks and sexual gymnastics so common in "how to" books about love.

Life-Design: Living Your Life by Choice Instead of Chance
This is a 106-page workbook based on a "life planning" course Peggy and James have conducted for the past 40 years.

Quotes about Peggy's Work

- Your efforts are systematically shedding more and more light on the topic of affairs. I am extremely appreciative of your efforts because I believe it is what is needed to get it out of the closet and into a place where it can be examined. It will make all the difference.

- You have a very nice treatment of an important subject—free from hyperbole and filled with understanding and compassion.

- What can I say! Astonishing! I have learned lots of good points other "experts" never touched.

- I applaud your work and feel fortunate to live in a time among people willing to tackle our important social problems, that in the long run affect the fabric of our society.

- Great information and perspectives! You are an incredible resource!

- The integrity of your web site is the best of any that I have found. Thank you for your fine work.

- It's such a relief to hear some "realistic" advice. It's just the kind of information I needed so desperately.

- Thank you so much for all your insight and information. You are a true source of comfort to me during this most difficult time.

- "Helpful" is not the word. You probably saved my marriage and my life.

- Thanks for all your hard work and dedication to helping those of us who are hurting.

- I've found your approach to be such a relief. Thank you for your level-headed approach.

- I'm so glad to see so much good information, well outlined and well presented for those who find themselves so lost in pain!

- Thank you for dealing with this subject in a way that represents the way society really is, rather than just condemn everyone who is involved in an affair.

- I could not have survived the first very difficult year without your wonderful insight.

- I can't thank you enough for all of the information on your site. You truly saved me, kept me sane during the first days after I found out about my husband's affair. You are right: reading and getting information—taking the rational approach— helped me when I was overwhelmed by emotion. Thank you from the bottom of my heart.

- Thank you for your work. The advice you have is exactly the kind of information I needed to hear.

- Your information has been a constant source of comfort and knowledge. More helpful than support group meetings, or counseling sessions.

151

Made in the USA
San Bernardino, CA
23 January 2020